British Railway Pict⟨

East Coast Main Line at Nationalisation

Michael Dove
C Eng MIMechE

Ian Allan
PUBLISHING

CONTENTS

First published 2006

ISBN (10) 0 7110 3133 9
ISBN (13) 978 0 7110 3133 3

All rights reserved. No part of this book may be
reproduced or transmitted in any form or by any
means, electronic or mechanical, including
photocopying, recording or by any information
storage and retrieval system, without permission
from the Publisher in writing.

© Michael Dove 2006

Published by Ian Allan Publishing

an imprint of Ian Allan Publishing Ltd, Hersham,
Surrey KT12 4RG
Printed in England by Ian Allan Printing Ltd,
Hersham, Surrey KT12 4RG

Code: 0609/B

Visit the Ian Allan Publishing website at
www.ianallanpublishing.com

Front cover: In June 1949 Class A4 No 60033
Seagull negotiates the Brafferton curves on the
non-stop 'Capitals Limited' service.

Back cover, top: Class A4 No 11 *Empire of
India* with a down 'Flying Scotsman' at
Newcastle in August 1947. *H. N. James /
Colour-Rail NE5*

Back cover, middle: LNER Class B1 4-6-0
No 1018 *Gnu* at York in apple green.
C. C. B. Herbert / Colour-Rail NE207

Back cover, bottom: LNER Class V2 2-6-2
No 60835 *The Green Howard, Alexandra,
Princess of Wales's Own Yorkshire Regiment*
under Holgate gantry, York station, 1949.
E. Sanderson / Colour-Rail BRE1134

Title page: Class A1 Pacific No 60134,
later to be named *Foxhunter*, with an up
'Yorkshire Pullman' during December 1948.
The somersault-type signals here were devised
by the Great Northern Railway to address
problems caused by freezing. These particular
signals were replaced by the much simpler
upper-quadrant type.

FOREWORD

There was a scene, long since gone from
King's Cross, that was repeated
frequently during the day and into the
night — the departure of an express
heading north behind one of Gresley's or
Peppercorn's   majestic   Pacific
locomotives; this could be an express
from Platform 10, bound for Aberdeen,
Edinburgh, Newcastle, Leeds or Hull,
maybe the 10am 'Flying Scotsman',
waiting to dive into Gasworks Tunnel
and climb through the London suburbs to
Hertfordshire and beyond. A similar
scene, also long gone, was enacted at
Waverley, in the heart of Edinburgh.
Here the departing train could be the
southbound 'Scotsman', with a Pacific
from Haymarket shed in charge, initially
heading east to the North Sea coast and
then turning south through the Borders
to Newcastle, York and London. In either
direction the passengers would be
relaxed, safe in the knowledge that the
train was being handled by a footplate
crew of many years' experience. The
stations along the way would be
populated by schoolboys, their Ian Allan
'ABCs' at the ready.

Today the East Coast main line still
has the 10am 'Scotsman', nowadays
powered by a clinically efficient Class
91 electric locomotive; this has enough
power to make light work of the climb
out of London and hurtle the train
between the two capitals in two hours
less, the passengers will still be happy
that there is a skilled driver at the
controls, and there is still the sense of
occasion engendered by a journey by
express train. But the special magic of
the steam era has gone. The great
stations   —   King's   Cross,   York,
Newcastle Central and Waverley, with
their high arching roofs designed to
disperse smoke — remain, substantially
unchanged. Maybe there is still the
faintest whiff of hot oil and sulphur. But
the schoolboy spotters have gone, and
the atmosphere of old, with simmering
engines and steam rising from carriage-
pipe connections, is no more.

For the railway historian the 1930s
were probably the years of greatest
significance for the East Coast main line.
They were notable for the non-stop
'Flying Scotsman' and for the emergence
of Gresley's 'A4s' and his celebrated
streamlined expresses, but the period
covered by this book —the late 1940s
and early 1950s — still held much of
interest. There was the reintroduction of
the apple-green and garter-blue liveries
— very welcome after the drab war years
— the 1948 Locomotive Exchanges, the
introduction   of   new   classes   of
locomotive (notably Pacifics), the
gradual return to something like
normality, with the Pullmans running
again, and more named trains. This book,
with its many photographs, will, it is
hoped, remind readers of those days
gone forever.

Acknowledgements

There are four people without whose
help this book would not have seen the
light of day — my brother, John, who
taught me about photography, George
Dow, who provided the lineside permits
(and of whom more anon), Peter Waller
of Ian Allan Publishing, who saw the
potential for such a book, and, last but by
no means least, my wife, Anne, whose
proofreading   and   encouragement
ensured its completion on time.

Michael Dove
Godmanchester
August 2006

*All photographs are by the author, unless
credited otherwise.*

Right: In 1923, the newly appointed
Chief Mechanical Engineer of the LNER,
H. N. Gresley, had this locomotive, Ivatt
Atlantic No 4419, fitted with a booster drive.
The idea was to provide extra power for
situations such as that encountered here,
the climb out of Kings Cross. The 1 in 107
gradient, immediately on leaving the station
and up through Gasworks and Copenhagen
tunnels, was a severe test for any locomotive
(by Finsbury Park, only 2½ miles out, the train
would have been lifted 120 ft). The booster
consisted of 2 cylinders driving onto the
trailing pair of wheels; its steam feed pipe can
be seen above the running plate. When in use,
the locomotive's tractive effort was increased
by nearly 50%, although it could only be used
at low speeds owing to its high steam
consumption. This photograph was taken
on 17 September 1928. *E. R. Wethersett*

THE EAST COAST MAIN LINE
A BRIEF HISTORY

The route of the East Coast main line follows quite closely that of the old Great North Road, which was, during the 18th and early 19th centuries, the principal route for stage coaches from London to the North East and Scotland. In the days before railways there needed to be a very pressing reason for people to subject themselves to an uncomfortable coach journey of two or three days, entailing overnight stops. Horses had to be changed about every 10 miles, so on a journey from, say, London to Newcastle there could be 25 changes, some 100 horses in all, resulting in frequent interruptions to a journey. Horse-changeover times varied greatly but could be less than 60 seconds,

conjuring up scenes akin to present-day Grand Prix pit-stops. Good stage coaches could average upwards of 10 miles an hour, mail coaches (which also carried passengers) a little more. However, the road coaches didn't stand a chance against the opening of through railway routes, permitting average speeds upwards of 40mph and offering much greater comfort, and soon most of their passengers had been attracted away.

Investors were queuing up to put their money into the development of new routes, none more so than routes north from London. So was born what was eventually to become the East Coast main line — a partnership between three

railways, the Great Northern, the Great Eastern and the North British. The Great Northern Railway, despite its name, reached only as far north as Doncaster. Its London terminus was originally at Maiden Lane (York Road), until King's Cross station was opened in 1852. In the early days a direct route to the north was spoiled by a long detour through Lincoln, but this all changed with the opening, also in 1852, of a direct route from Peterborough via Grantham, Newark and Retford to Doncaster; known as the 'Towns Line', it was so called to differentiate it from the previous route through open country with few settlements of any size.

The North Eastern Railway also made improvements. In 1871 a new route from Shaftholme Junction, 5 miles north of Doncaster, to York via Selby was opened (superseding a route through Knottingley and Church Fenton), and in 1872 a direct route to Newcastle via Chester-le-Street and the Team Valley was completed. These changes also brought additional benefits: the new lines being constructed were designed with better alignments and gradients, it having become obvious that speeds higher than those envisaged when the earlier lines were built would become the norm.

The North British Railway continued the route north from Berwick to Edinburgh and beyond to Aberdeen over the Forth and Tay bridges. The section of line between Belford and Dunbar is the one stretch on the entire route from King's Cross that can accurately be titled East Coast, running for some distance alongside (or very near) the North Sea. It also has the most formidable gradient — the 4 miles at 1 in 96 of Cockburnspath Bank.

It was becoming apparent that all these changes to the East Coast route were bringing it into direct competition with that of the London & North Western Railway and Caledonian Railway to Scotland from the former's London terminus, Euston, less than half a mile down the road from King's Cross. So began what was to be a period of intense competition between the West and East Coast routes between London and Edinburgh, culminating in the 'Race to the North', with each side continually bettering its rival's times. When it became clear that the situation was getting dangerous and unlikely to show a clear winner a truce was called, agreement being reached on a minimum journey time

Left: In July 1937 the LNER introduced the second of its streamlined expresses, the superlative 'Coronation'. The sumptuous coaches were air-conditioned with a high level of sound-proofing. The exterior, if anything, was even more striking, the carriage sides being finished in two shades of blue enamel. Carriage lettering was formed in stainless steel. Class A4s were always the motive power provided; on Cockburnspath bank, some 40 miles north of the Scotland-England border, we see a southbound No 4491 *Commonwealth of Australia* on 24 August 1937. *E. R. Wethersett*

Right: The 10.0am departure of the non-stop 'Flying Scotsman' from Edinburgh's Waverley station always generated much interest; this Friday 20 August 1937 scene shows two-month-old 'A4' No 4492 *Dominion of New Zealand*. The relief crew will be sitting in the front compartment of the leading carriage, having a 3½-hour rest before taking over for the second half of the journey to Kings Cross. The coaching stock, although having the traditional teak finish, was specially designed and built for this service, with additional features including a barber's shop and cocktail bar. *E. R. Wethersett*

from London to Edinburgh of 8¼ hours. Surprisingly this agreement would stand until 1932, despite such developments as restaurant cars, a succession of more powerful locomotives and the widespread introduction of water troughs.

The East Coast main line now settled into a period of relative stability up to and beyond the amalgamation in 1923 of the three constituent companies into the London & North Eastern Railway. Then, in 1928, the LNER gave notice that the status quo was to end by scheduling the 'Flying Scotsman' express to make the run from King's Cross to Edinburgh Waverley without a stop. It was the longest non-stop run in the world and was the first of a series of publicity coups by the LNER during the following years. March 1935 saw a record-breaking demonstration run by 'A3' Pacific *Papyrus*, followed in September of the same year by the introduction of a streamlined express, the 'Silver Jubilee', which ran between King's Cross and Newcastle. In 1937, following the success of this train, two further streamliners were introduced — the 'Coronation' (King's Cross–Edinburgh Waverley) and the 'West Riding Limited' (King's Cross–Leeds/Bradford). To crown it all was the record-breaking run in 1938 when *Mallard* set the world speed record for steam traction at 126mph, which has never been beaten.

The main architects of these schemes were H. N. Gresley (knighted in 1936), the

Chief Mechanical Engineer, and Sir Ralph Wedgwood, the Chief General Manager. It reflects great credit on them that they managed to bring them to fruition during a period of severe financial restraint. Their initiatives brought the LNER, and in particular the East Coast main line, into the limelight with immense press coverage at a time when the railways were still the pre-eminent form of transport. A never-to-be-forgotten experience was the sight of one of Gresley's streamlined expresses at speed. These were indeed halcyon days for the East Coast main line.

The outbreak of war in 1939 brought an abrupt end to any thoughts of further developments, and the railways again came under Government control, as they had during World War 1. The LNER headquarters were transferred from King's Cross and Liverpool Street to a country house in Hertfordshire, as it was expected that London stations would become targets for air attack. Sir Nigel Gresley, who had set up an office at King's Cross when he became Chief Mechanical Engineer of the LNER in 1923, moved to his home at Watton-at-Stone, also in Hertfordshire, and operated from there until his death in 1941. Both King's Cross and Liverpool Street did indeed suffer, particularly during an air raid in May 1941, when they were both badly damaged. Among other important stations to suffer was York, severely damaged in April of the

following year during a 'Baedeker' raid, so called because the Luftwaffe High Command decided to bomb historic British towns and cities chosen by referring to a German publication, Baedeker's Tourist Guide to Britain.

In spite of a depleted workforce, reduced by more than 100,000 to the armed forces, the railways rose to the challenge of the massive extra demands put on them by the war. The building of some new locomotives was permitted because there was an acute shortage of mixed-traffic locomotives, but because most of the workshops had been largely turned over to the manufacture of munitions (for example, the LNER made, among other armaments, more than 3½ million bombs and shells), capacity to maintain rolling-stock was scant. Track wear and tear was exacerbated by the greatly increased wartime traffic coupled with an acute shortage of maintenance personnel. More than five years of war took a heavy toll, and in 1945 track condition was at an all-time low.

A blanket speed limit of 60mph had been in force since 1939, and this continued until 1946, when it was raised on the East Coast main line to 70mph (apart from King's Cross–Hatfield, where it remained at 60). A start was made on improvements, but there was still a massive backlog of maintenance work to be tackled, and it took some years and into

Nationalisation before it again reached a satisfactory standard.

As track conditions improved, thoughts turned to the reinstatement of the Pullman and streamlined expresses that had been taken out of service in August 1939, before hostilities began, and stored in Scotland and the North of England. It was decided to delay reintroduction of the streamliners until conditions improved to a point where they could run at something approaching their prewar speeds; all three had timings that demanded average speeds appreciably higher than those of the normal expresses. The 'Coronation', for instance, had the highest speed scheduled in the country, an average of 71.9mph for the run between King's Cross and York. During the summer of 1947 the then Chief General Manager, Sir Charles Newton, who had been among the keenest to see the three streamliners running again, again pressed that consideration be given to the matter. As it was, Nationalisation overtook events, and they never ran again. It is open to conjecture whether the decision would have been the same had Gresley still been alive.

The Pullmans, which relied more on luxury than speed for their custom, were brought back in the years 1946-8. The 'Yorkshire Pullman' was the first, revived in November 1946, but it ran for only three months before being withdrawn again, due to a fuel crisis brought on by a period of very severe weather. This was the time when, for a short period, coal trains were given precedence over all other traffic, a unique event. The 'Yorkshire Pullman' ran again from October 1947, and the 'Queen of Scots' came back in July 1948. An additional train, the 'Tees–Tyne Pullman', was introduced in September 1948, ironically almost replicating the service provided previously by the 'Silver Jubilee', apart from longer journey times.

The 'Flying Scotsman' was again reinstated as a non-stop express between King's Cross and Edinburgh but reverted to calling at Peterborough, York, Newcastle and Berwick when a new non-stop service, the 'Capitals Limited', was introduced in May 1949. However, these non-stop runs were coming under threat, as they involved loco crews' spending nights away from home (known as 'lodging turns'), as did many other services, including express freight trains. They were relatively common in the 1930s, but attitudes were changing, and the train crews' trade union, the Associated Society of Locomotive Engineers and Firemen (ASLEF), was pressing for them to be greatly reduced and ultimately abolished.

In the earliest days of the railways drivers were drawn from skilled engineering backgrounds (for instance, the Stockton & Darlington's *Locomotion* was driven by George Stephenson's elder brother, who had been closely associated with him during the railway's development), and they enjoyed high status and remuneration. With rapid expansion came a need for many more drivers than were available from engineering sources, and this caused a lowering of their recognition and status. Also, over the years their increased responsibilities and workloads, brought about by more powerful locomotives and higher speeds, was not properly acknowledged, and it was the discontent that this generated that had resulted in the formation of ASLEF in 1880. ASLEF was one of three rail unions and has vigorously fought the footplatemen's corner since those early days. One example of the lack of consideration shown to drivers and firemen was the inexplicable notion that they should not be provided with seating on the footplate. It was not until the 1920s that Gresley pioneered the fitting of seats in cabs — and the 1930s before they became generally accepted. Another example was the very poor hostel facilities provided for 'lodging turn'

Left: After the war the 'Yorkshire Pullman' returned for just three months from November 1946, then again from October 1947. The up service is seen heading through the bleak and cold Nottinghamshire countryside behind 'A1' No 60119 in the early afternoon of 5 January 1949. The locomotive was subsequently named *Patrick Stirling*, after the Locomotive Superintendent of the Great Northern Railway from 1866 to 1895. The 'Yorkshire Pullman' quite often had a luggage van marshalled at the front of the train.

Below left: The 'Queen of Scots' Pullman was reintroduced in July 1948. On 12 January 1949, having just descended the 1-in-178 gradient of Gamston Bank, the northbound service slows for the 65mph speed restriction at Retford Crossing. Gresley 'A3' No 60098 *Spion Kop* is immaculately clean, as was usual on this turn, and is sporting the new 'Queen of Scots' headboard; this was cast in aluminium and replaced the old prewar type, which was a plate formed from sheet metal with a painted inscription that looked decidedly tatty after long usage.

Above right: A new express service, the 'Tees-Tyne Pullman', was introduced in September 1948. Here a very dirty 'A4' Pacific, No 60013 *Dominion of New Zealand*, heads the southbound train past the Grove Road level crossing near Retford, during the spring of 1951. *Dominion of New Zealand* was one of a group of five 'A4s' named after Commonwealth countries and allocated to the 'Coronation' streamlined express, which ran between Kings Cross and Edinburgh from 1937 to the outbreak of World War 2.
The coaches of this train would be washed by hand at the end of each journey and the locomotive would be equally immaculate. Its cleanliness then would be in sharp contrast to that at the time of this photograph.

Right: A new non-stop service, the 'Capitals Limited' was introduced between King's Cross and Edinburgh in May 1949 (becoming the 'Elizabethan' following the Coronation of HM Queen Elizabeth in 1953). During the 1950s this service superseded the 'Flying Scotsman' as the Eastern Region's premier express. Its non-stop run between Kings Cross and Edinburgh was made possible by the corridor tenders fitted to some of the 'A3s' and 'A4s', enabling the engine crews to be changed at half distance. No.60010 *Dominion of Canada* is seen here near Ketton Hall, County Durham, hauling the northbound train on 28 May 1949, during the week of its inauguration. The bell on the smoke box was presented to the LNER by the Canadian Pacific Railway, as was the 5-chime whistle.

crews; one of the major grievances was that crews were not provided with decent comfortable accommodation while away from home.

The worth of the footplatemen has become more apparent since the demise of the steam locomotive and with the realisation of how they had to cope with very difficult and onerous conditions. These included poor visibility (sometimes compounded by drifting smoke and steam, and made even more serious by the lack of advance-warning systems) and extremes of temperature in the cab, laced with generous amounts of coal dust and sometimes almost intolerable conditions in tunnels, particularly at low speeds. The visibility problem was one that Oliver Bulleid, Chief Mechanical Engineer of the

Southern Railway, had addressed in the late 1940s with his 'Leader'-class locomotive, which had a cab at both ends and would have cured the visibility problem at a stroke. However, the design was not a success owing to major mechanical problems, and it never went into service.

In view of the footplatemen's lack of proper recognition it is even more remarkable that 'Top Link' drivers and firemen in particular were noted for their professionalism and dedication. Drivers such as Bill Sparshatt, Ted Hailstone, Arthur Taylor, Bill Hoole and many others will be remembered with respect and affection as long as the steam days on the East Coast main line are talked about.

NATIONALISATION

In July 1945 the fate of the London & North Eastern Railway was sealed. The war in Europe was over (and that in the Far East had but a month to run), and a General Election called by Winston Churchill had just voted into power, by an overwhelming majority, a Labour Government.

The Wartime Coalition had done its job. The British people, both those who had fought and civilians, had just endured five years of sacrifice and hardship and felt empowered to demand a change away from the divisive prewar class system. It was against this background that the new Government embarked on a programme of sweeping social reforms. The National Health Service was formed, and wholesale Nationalisation was planned. This included taking into public ownership the coal and steel industries, power, the road haulage industry (which became British Road Services), canals and, of course, the railways.

Nationalisation was strenuously opposed by the railway hierarchy, although the shareholders were, in the main, less hostile, as they had had a pretty raw deal over many years (none more so than those of the LNER, which had never made a profit during the 25 years of its existence). When it became obvious that the Government had made up its mind that the railways were moving into public ownership, proposals were mooted by the railways that would have enabled the current management to continue more or less independently. The idea put forward was that the buildings, track and ancillary equipment be sold to the state but that locomotives and rolling-stock should remain with the existing owners, which would run them as before but under franchise (somewhat similar in concept to the arrangements implemented by John Major's Conservative Government in 1994, when the railways were privatised). Sir Ronald Matthews, the LNER Chairman, tried to co-ordinate an approach of all the railway companies to the Government, but without success, and when the proposals were finally put to the Minister of Transport they were dismissed out of hand. The Transport Act 1947 was passed, and the date set for railway nationalisation was 1 January 1948, giving very little time for the railway industry to recover from the pounding it had received during the war years.

On the formation of British Railways the LNER was split into three distinct regions, two of which were similar geographically to the companies existing before the 1923 Grouping. The Eastern Region covered an area similar to that of the old Great Northern, Great Central and Great Eastern railways, while the North Eastern Region took in the lines of the old North Eastern Railway. The Scottish Region encompassed the operations of both the LMS and LNER north of the border.

Railway employees were almost unanimously in favour of Nationalisation, as it was making it 'their railway'. At midnight on the appointed day drivers and firemen up and down the country sounded their locomotive whistles, and there was a general feeling of anticipation. As it turned out the only apparent change for a long time was the replacement of the individual railways' identities on buildings, uniforms and rolling-stock with 'British Railways' or 'BR'.

There was one event, however, that aroused widespread public interest: the Locomotive Exchanges. Arrangements for these were started almost immediately after Nationalisation, and the first exchanges took place, after a remarkably short preparation time, in mid-April 1948. The object was to evaluate similar types of locomotives from the four constituent companies by running on each other's metals, which would hopefully throw up some useful comparisons of performance and efficiency for use in future developments. There were three groups: express passenger, mixed traffic and freight. On the Eastern Region the express-passenger locomotives were trialled on the East Coast main line between London and Leeds, being rostered north from London on the 1.10pm King's Cross–Leeds Central and returning the next morning on the 7.50am from Leeds. Other Eastern Region routes were Marylebone–Manchester London Road for mixed-traffic locomotives and Ferme Park–Peterborough for freight locomotives.

This was not the first time that the East Coast main line had played host to locomotive exchanges. A previous occasion had come about as a result of a claim by the GWR that its Collett-designed 'Castle'-class 4-6-0s were more powerful than Gresley's 'A1' Pacifics.

Left: The 1948 Locomotive Exchanges. The Great Western 'King' design was 11 years older than the next-oldest entrant in the express-passenger category, the LNER's 'A4' Pacific. No 6018 *King Henry VI*, still sporting the GWR crest on its tender, is seen here on a familiarisation run at Babworth Road bridge, Retford, on 12 May. It was unfortunate that, because of clearance problems across the width of the cylinders, the loading gauges of the Southern and London Midland regions could not accommodate the 'Kings', so the East Coast main line was their only 'foreign' route.

Above: No 6018, with the LNER dynamometer car, sweeps down Gamston Bank on a test run in mid-May with the 1.10pm King's Cross–Leeds express.

Right: Bulleid's Merchant Navy' Pacifics were nominated as the Southern Region's representatives in the express-passenger group. They needed to be fitted with tenders that had water pick-up scoops, as the Southern Region had no water troughs. Here No 35019 *French Line CGT*, with an ex-LMS tender, is seen near Grove on a familiarisation run during May.

Below: Another 'Merchant Navy', No 35017 *Belgian Marine*, at the head of the 1.10pm King's Cross– Leeds express during the last week in May, passing beneath Babworth Road bridge, Retford.

Above: Driver Brooker of Camden shed on the footplate of London Midland Region 'Rebuilt Royal Scot' 4-6-0 No 46162 *Queen's Westminster Riflemen*, still carrying its pre-Nationalisation tender lettering and heading the 1.10pm King's Cross–Leeds express, on 29 April 1948. The leading coach is the LNER dynamometer car, an indication that this is a test rather than a familiarisation run.

Left: The LMR's 'Duchess' representative was No 46236 *City of Bradford*. It was consistently outperformed by its smaller 'Royal Scot' stablemate but was the only locomotive to complete the express-passenger trials trouble-free. It is seen at Babworth Road Bridge, Retford, during the last week of April.

The claim was made at the British Empire Exhibition of 1924, held at Wembley, where, in the Palace of Engineering, the two types were exhibited virtually side by side by their respective companies, the 'Castle' displaying a notice claiming it to be the most powerful express passenger locomotive in Britain. This was something that many people, judging by the difference in size, found hard to believe, but a theoretical calculation of tractive effort revealed it to be so.

Tractive effort was a figure commonly quoted by locomotive manufacturers as part of their published specification. It is a theoretical figure derived from a formula using measurements relating to the number of cylinders, their swept volume, maximum boiler pressure and driving-wheel diameter. A more meaningful indicator of performance is drawbar pull, which is measured (by means of a dynamometer car) from a locomotive while working. This pull is dependent on the actual work done by the cylinders, which, in turn, is influenced by (among other things) the degree of superheat, the streamlining of steam passages and the efficiency of the cylinder valves. All of these factors affect the pressure drop between boiler and cylinders, and this determines the cylinder thrust available. Maintaining this power output is dependent on the ability of the firebox and boiler to produce continuously the required quality and quantity of steam. Maximum power is most commonly attained during acceleration and/or climbing.

A dynamometer car is a vehicle specially designed for measuring and recording locomotive performance. In use it is marshalled between the locomotive and the rest of the train and measures the actual pull between the locomotive and the train (the drawbar pull). This figure and the speed at the time can be used to calculate the horsepower developed. It should be noted that this is not the actual power developed (as it does not include that required to accelerate and/or lift — if on a gradient — the locomotive itself, which, of course, will not show up on the drawbar) but represents the useful power available to drive the train.

It was agreed to compare the two locomotives exhibited at the British Empire Exhibition by operating, in conditions as near as possible identical, on each other's lines, and these trials were

Left and Below: City of Bradford again, heading north through Retford on one of the familiarisation runs, and pulling away from Retford with the 7.50am Leeds Central–King's Cross express.

conducted during the summer of 1925 with two weeks of test running. The GWR locomotive came out the undisputed winner both in water and coal consumption and overall performance. Particularly impressive was the ease with which the 'Castle' tackled the notoriously difficult climb from the start at King's Cross up through Gasworks and Copenhagen tunnels to Finsbury Park.

As a result of this exchange Gresley decided to make modifications to improve his Pacifics. The most significant of these was changing from short- to long-travel cylinder valves. A later development was to increase the boiler pressure by 20%, and these changes formed the basis of a new class, 'A3'. Subsequently all the 'A1s' (later reclassified 'A10', the top spot having been taken by Edward Thompson's

new Pacific) were rebuilt to this specification, but not that speedily, the last not being done until 1948, some 20 years later!

Dynamometer cars naturally played a big part in the post-Nationalisation Locomotive Exchanges of 1948. Test results in these exchanges were very mixed, partly because loco crews were not given any clear guidance of what was required of them. Some crews concentrated on keeping to the timetable, while others were more concerned with coal consumption. A few things stood out: the London Midland Region's 'Rebuilt Royal Scot', in the capable hands of Driver Brooker of Camden shed, regularly outperformed its more powerful 'Duchess' stablemate. However, in mitigation the 'Duchess' entered for the

exchanges, *City of Bradford*, was the only express-passenger locomotive to complete the trials without a hitch. The Eastern Region 'A4s' put in some excellent performances, but these were overshadowed by no fewer than three failures of the middle cylinder's big end, the locomotives' Achilles heel.

While the exchanges were still taking place Robert Riddles, as the newly appointed Member of the Railway Executive for Mechanical & Electrical Engineering (in effect British Railways' Chief Engineer), had already set out specifications for new BR locomotives, and design work was in progress. It is doubtful whether the Locomotive Exchanges were to have much (if any) effect on future designs, as Riddles had already decided to concentrate on

Left: A typically dirty 'Austerity' 2-8-0, No 90122, working hard on the slow line as it attacks Gamston Bank with a mixed goods. The photograph dates from early 1951, by which time the majority of heavy goods trains on this part of the East Coast main line were hauled by 'Austerities'. They were designed during World War 2 under the direction of Robert Riddles, an LMS man who had been appointed to the Ministry of Supply. His remit was to produce a freight locomotive for use on the Continent after D-Day, and this he did in conjunction with the North British Locomotive Co, Glasgow, which as well as manufacturing the locomotives carried out the design work. The 'Austerities' were an immediate success, and, in all, more than 900 were built; they were some of the last steam locomotives to remain in service with British Railways. The LNER purchased 200 of them from the War Department in 1946 and later, after Nationalisation, another 269 were loaned to the Eastern Region by the Ministry of Supply.

Above left: It was unusual to be able to read the cabside numbers of 'Austerities', most of which looked as though they had never been cleaned. Here No 90597 heads a trainload of empty wagons back to the Nottinghamshire coalfields. These coal trains were one of the major sources of income for the Eastern and North Eastern Regions. British Railways' annual consumption of coal before the arrival of diesels was more than 2 million tons a year, keeping nearly 30,000 miners in employment, and the loss of this business was a significant factor in the eventual demise of the coal industry in this country.

Above right: Two Riddles 'Austerities', with characteristically illegible numbers, passing on the East Coast main line. The design of these 2-8-0s dispensed with the usual asbestos-mattress insulation and instead simply used an air gap. However, damaged or ill-fitting cladding around the boiler, as here, could reduce the effectiveness of this method of insulation. *John Dove*

Left: A coal train heads south towards Darlington during April 1949 with one of the North Eastern Railway's 'Q6' locomotives in charge; 15 months after Nationalisation, the tender and cabside of No 3357 still show no evidence of this. The 'Q6' class was designed under the direction of Sir Vincent Raven and built at the NER works at Darlington from 1913. The type was one of the mainstays on goods traffic in the North East; some 120 were built, and with a tractive effort of 30,000lb they were well able to cope with the heavy gradients of the Northumberland and County Durham mineral lines.

Above: An unidentified Robinson 'O4' 2-8-0 heads a northbound freight train in wintry conditions at the beginning of 1949 near Sutton, in north Nottinghamshire. *John Dove*

Above right: The various 0-6-0 classes were commonly seen workhorses. 'J11' No 64335, of a GCR design dating back to 1901, is seen running light on its way back to its shed at Retford. *John Dove*

Below: With the completion of the 49 Peppercorn 'A1s', Gresley's Pacifics, although still very much in evidence on the leading expresses, were often available for more workaday tasks. Here, in August 1950, No 60032 *Gannet* heads the 2.55pm fish train from Hull to London. There was no mistaking these trains, as they were characterised by their own special fish smell which, on a still day, could linger for some time after the train had passed.

straightforward, easily maintained motive power, as exemplified by the excellent 'Austerity' locomotives, the specification for which he had drawn up during his stint in charge of the wartime Directorate of Transportation Equipment.

Freight had always been a very important part of traffic on the East Coast main line and was its major source of income. In the 1940s and '50s the 'Austerity' locomotives became the preferred motive power for hauling heavy goods trains, but older classes were still extensively used, including Raven 'Q6' 0-8-0s (mainly in the North East), and Robinson 'O4' 2-8-0s and their Thompson

rebuilds, the 'O1s'. Two of the major commodities carried were coal, from the North East and the East Midlands, and fish, notably from Aberdeen and Grimsby but also from Hull, Whitby and Scarborough. Of all the railway companies the LNER had always carried by far the greatest levels of fish traffic. By way of example, in 1949/50 there were 11 of these trains despatched each day from Hull. A feature of fish trains was the necessity to transport the cargo, being perishable, at virtually express-passenger speeds. To this end they were always continuously braked, a feature pioneered by the Great Northern Railway. Gresley's

ubiquitous 'V2s' often hauled these trains, as did Pacifics in later years.

During 1948 the East Coast main line became the victim of some of the worst damage ever suffered by a railway line in Britain. In August unprecedented rainfall in the Lammermuir Hills caused floodwater to wash away no fewer than seven bridges and cause several major landslides on the line between Berwick and Dunbar. As a result trains were diverted by various routes, but remarkably it took only three months for temporary bridges to be built and the line to reopen. However, it took until May 1950 for these bridges to be replaced by permanent structures.

MOTIVE POWER

The East Coast main line approached Nationalisation with a stud of potentially highly competent Gresley types, although they needed good maintenance to keep them running efficiently — something that was only now beginning to pick up after eight years of making do. Sir Nigel Gresley had been a charismatic leader as Chief Mechanical Engineer since the Grouping in 1923, and his death in 1941 robbed the LNER of a pre-eminent locomotive engineer who was held in the highest esteem by his directors and by those who worked with and for him. He had an excellent engineering and design team based at Doncaster, and although his headquarters was at King's Cross he spent a lot of time with his close-knit team of draughtsmen in the Doncaster drawing office, where almost all the design work was executed. He had the advantage that he was able to travel by train between the two sites almost literally door to door, and it was not unknown for a through express to make an unscheduled stop at Doncaster for his benefit!

Below: For many years the Ivatt Atlantics successfully worked East Coast expresses, No 2877 being seen towards the end of its working days on a summer evening in 1947. It would be withdrawn in November 1949, to be used as a stationary boiler for about two years before being scrapped.

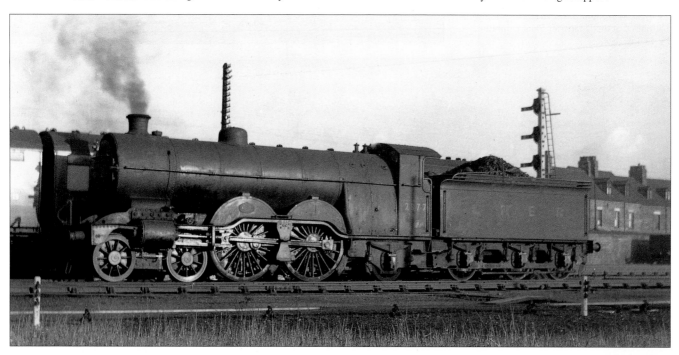

Above: No 251 was Ivatt's prototype 'Large Atlantic', built in 1902 as the first of that very successful class of locomotives. It was withdrawn in November 1947, and its restoration had only just been completed in time for this Doncaster Plant exhibition held in July 1948. Latterly LNER No 2800, the locomotive is here seen with its original Great Northern number.

Above: Class D49 4-4-0 No 62746 *The Middleton* running light back to Darlington on 19 February 1949. These locomotives, built in the late 1920s, numbered 76 in total and were generally based in the North of England and Scotland. Forty of them, including this example, were named after famous hunts, their nameplates distinguished by the figure of a fox above the name. An unusual feature of these plates was that, because it was decided that the fox should point forwards on both sides, the foxes were handed and bolted in place, to enable the same design of nameplate to be used.

Right: The first Gresley Pacific built as an 'A3', which entered service as No 2743 *Felstead* in 1928. A batch of 10 locomotives was built that year, to be followed by further batches in 1930 and 1934.

Below: The iconic Gresley streamlined 'A4', fresh from overhaul in early BR guise: The footplate of No 60029 *Woodcock* is being well patronised at the Doncaster Plant exhibition on 17 July 1948.

Below: Class A4 Pacific No 60034 at Retford shed on 9 January 1949, having failed on a through express. This was the last of the final batch of four 'A4s' built, in 1938, the only examples fitted from new with the Kylchap double-blastpipe and chimney. These chimneys, which were to become commonplace on larger BR Standard locomotives, originated when a Finnish engineer, Kyosti Kylala, designed a multi-stream exhaust system to reduce sparks from the chimney, an important feature in a country of forests. It was found that, as well as reducing sparking, these chimneys gave a more even draught over the boiler tubeplate, increasing boiler efficiency and also reducing the frequency of boiler tube cleaning. André Chapelon, the celebrated French locomotive engineer, refined the design, and the name 'Kylchap' was coined from the two surnames.

Gresley was succeeded by Edward Thompson, who was promoted from the post of Mechanical Engineer, Doncaster. Thompson had spent much of his career being answerable to Gresley, and the relationship was at times strained. His appointment as Chief Mechanical Engineer was greeted with foreboding by those who had been close to Gresley. Among the changes that Thompson made, justifying their fears, was the redeployment of key personnel away from Doncaster, thus breaking up the well-established engineering team.

Thompson's first new design was the Class B1 4-6-0 mixed-traffic locomotive, and the prototype was completed in December 1942. It was one of the few new designs allowed under a Ministry of Supply directive specifying that only in exceptional circumstances were new models to be allowed. The 'B1s' continued to be produced until 1952 and eventually numbered 410. They were a very successful and versatile class and were used throughout the Eastern, North Eastern and Scottish regions of British Railways.

Thompson was keen to build Pacifics and achieved this, despite the bar on new designs, by rebuilding Gresley's six Class P2 2-8-2s as 4-6-2s, these rebuilds becoming Class A2/2. These locomotives, originally built in 1934 for service on the difficult part of the East Coast main line north of Edinburgh, with its heavy gradients, are always identified with the first of the class, *Cock o' the North*.

Owing to a very serious shortage of motive power, brought about by a huge increase in all types of traffic, the LNER had continued to build the highly regarded Class V2 'Green Arrow' mixed-traffic locomotives during the war. Thompson managed to get the last four of the order completed as Pacifics to his design, these becoming Class A2/1. He achieved this by means of a not uncommon ploy (used in industry even today) to get around directives barring new projects: the work was done under the guise of improvements to an existing design.

An even more striking example of getting a new design spirited through was the controversial 'rebuild' of Gresley's first Pacific *Great Northern*, which became Class A1/1 and was intended to be the first of a new class of express-passenger locomotives. Virtually no existing components were used, and

Above: Thompson's first new design was the Class B1 4-6-0 mixed-traffic locomotive. Looking smart in LNER apple-green livery, No 1211 stands by the GN shed at Retford in 1950.

Right: The sole surviving Class B3 4-6-0, LNER No 1497, at the head of a local stopping train in the spring of 1948.

Left: Gresley Class V2 'Green Arrow' mixed-traffic 2-6-2 No 60918 heads north through County Durham with a King's Cross–Glasgow express during May 1949. The 'V2s' were used successfully on many of the East Coast expresses, although there was a short period in 1946 when they were subject to a speed restriction following two occasions when the front pony truck became derailed. Track condition was considered to be largely to blame, but as a precaution a modification was made to the pony-truck spring control.

Left: Mid-afternoon on 23 July 1949 'V2' No 60960 breasts the summit near Markham at the head of a relief passenger train for Doncaster. The class totalled 184, more than 100 of which were built during the war to alleviate a serious shortage of mixed-traffic locomotives. No 60960 was turned out in November 1942 from Darlington Works, where all but 25 of the class were built.

Below: The first of Thompson's 'L1' 2-6-4T locomotives was built at Doncaster in May 1945, numbered 9000 and turned out in LNER green; the next 29 were constructed at Darlington in 1948, followed by others built by contractors. No 9000 is seen at Gateshead on 25 July 1946. *E. R. Wethersett*

Left: No 60508 *Duke of Rothesay*, one of Thompson's 'A2/1' Pacifics, built at Doncaster in 1944. In July 1948 this locomotive was involved in an unusual accident at New Southgate while approaching King's Cross with an Edinburgh express. Due to a fault in the track the rear pony truck became derailed at about 60mph, and a chain reaction resulted in the locomotive turning on its side and sliding along for some distance, coming to rest about ¼ mile from the initial derailment. It is seen here in the late spring of 1950 with a down express, its reporting number flapping in the wind, passing under London Road bridge at Grove near Retford.

effectively *Great Northern* was scrapped. About the only thing used was the name, but even the nameplates had to be re-cast, as there were no wheel splashers on which to mount the original curved design! It would have cost less and used less manpower to build a new locomotive from scratch, as well as increasing the motive-power stock by one. However, it must be said in mitigation that components of the old Great Northern were available as spares for the rest of the class.

When the bar on new projects was lifted a new design based on the 'A2/1' and 'A2/2' rebuilds was put into production, and this became Class A2. There was also a completely new tank locomotive, designated Class L1, and this was put into series production both at LNER Darlington and at subcontractors Vulcan Foundry and Robert Stephenson & Hawthorn. Thompson retired in June 1946 while his 'A2s' were in production. Fifteen were built in all, but they were never popular with motive-power depots or footplate crews, mainly due to poor reliability.

Thompson's successor was Arthur Peppercorn, a 'Gresley man', and he and the Assistant CME, Frank Harrison, set about improving the 'A2s'. Many changes were made, and these were incorporated in new production, following on immediately from the batch of 15 Thompson 'A2s'. It was very easy to tell them apart, because the Peppercorn versions had the outside cylinders moved forward from immediately ahead of the driving wheels to between the bogie wheels. Again, 15 locomotives were built.

Peppercorn and Harrison also introduced a new Pacific with larger driving wheels — 6ft 8in as opposed to the 6ft 2in of the 'A2s' — and these were classified 'A1'. Numbering 49 locomotives, built at both Doncaster and Darlington in 1948/9, they became a very common sight on the East Coast main line after Nationalisation and were reckoned by some to be the best express locomotives to be produced in Britain. Together with the Gresley 'A3s', 'A4s' and 'V2s' the Peppercorn 'A1s' and 'A2s' continued to handle with distinction the line's express passenger and goods trains until the arrival of the diesel-electrics.

Left: Class A2 *A. H. Peppercorn*, the first of the Peppercorn developments of the class and the last locomotive to be built at Doncaster before Nationalisation, still carrying its LNER number while on display at the 1948 Doncaster Plant exhibition. It was said that the plan was to name the locomotive Arthur Peppercorn but that the smoke-deflectors were too short.

Below: Most likely the first time that well-known preserved 'A2' No 60532 *Blue Peter* was photographed. It is seen ambling up Gamston Bank, with regulator barely open, on 24 March 1948, having just left Doncaster Plant on its running-in trials to Barkston Junction and back.

Right: Peppercorn's 'A1' class making its first appearance at the Doncaster Plant exhibition held in July 1948, a month before No 60114's official completion date. The class continued to be built until December of the following year, at both Doncaster and Darlington, and numbered 49 in total. They were the last locomotives of LNER design to be introduced, but notwithstanding they were all unfortunately broken up. However, there is currently an ambitious project to reproduce an 'A1', which at the time of writing is being built at Darlington by the A1 Steam Locomotive Trust and due for completion in 2007. The boy seen here standing on the front of the locomotive would not be allowed to do so today under Health & Safety regulations, while the four boys clambering on the tender would probably cause a major panic!

Above: Peppercorn 'A1' No 60116 was a regular on the southbound 'Tees–Tyne Pullman' from the train's inauguration in September 1948. This class immediately became popular with footplate crews and earned an enviable reputation for reliability. The mass of steam that collected round the chimney was something that was only usually seen in very cold conditions, as here at Ordsall on a bitter and murky day in January 1949. The effectiveness of the smoke-deflectors is also evident.

THE PHOTOGRAPHS

The author's photographs included here were taken primarily in the two years following nationalisation, 1948 and 1949. The inspiration for them came from the work of three great railway photographers of the prewar and early postwar era: Canon Eric Treacy, whose early favourite locations — Edge Hill (Liverpool) and Shap Fell — became familiar to many, Maurice W. Earley, who took some superb photographs in Sonning Cutting, near Reading, and T. Gordon Hepburn, who photographed the East Coast main line in and around Grantham. Also included are photographs from the collections of John Dove (the author's brother) and, in order to provided more complete coverage of the route, of that master railway photographer, Ernest Wethersett.

At the time there was still a shortage of photographic equipment and materials, especially cameras capable of taking good-quality photographs of trains in motion. However, there was an abundance of war-surplus materials, including aerial cameras with very high-quality lenses. The decision was made to incorporate one of these lenses, together with the camera's focal plane shutter, into a custom-built camera.

The lens chosen was a 7in-focal-length F2.5 Kodak Aero Ektar, and the focal-plane shutter was capable of 1/900sec

exposure times. The camera incorporated a 'swing back', a feature not often come across today; its purpose was to enable one side of the image to be focussed differently from the other, and it was achieved by tilting the axis of the lens (a swing front) or by tilting the film or plate (a swing back).

Large apertures were often necessary due to the relatively slow speed of the film emulsions available at the time, but of course large apertures give a small depth of focus. A swing-back facility enabled both ends of a three-quarter view of a train to be in focus; this also had the added advantage that the front of the train would be thrown into relief, with its background partially out of focus. A 7in lens was chosen because it gave a reasonable degree of perspective.

The camera used 3½ in x 2½ in glass plates, Kodak P1200 or Ilford HP3, the two giving similar results. Over the years they have not always been stored in ideal conditions but have survived remarkably well; unlike a third plate used, the Barnet Press. These became unprintable, but fortunately not many of that type were used.

Colour photography of moving trains was not then a viable proposition. Although colour films were beginning to become available the slowness of their emulsions was such that arresting motion was possible only if the train was moving very slowly. For example Dufaycolor, one of the very few types of colour film available, required an exposure of 30

times longer than, say, Ilford HP3 film or plate. A typical exposure time for a moving train would be 1/900sec; in a similar situation and with the same lens aperture the Dufaycolor film would require 1/30sec, in which time a train travelling at 60mph would have covered about 3ft — clearly unacceptable.

There was another problem with colour films: processing. Developers — and other solutions required — had to be made up with chemicals obtained from specialist suppliers; there were not yet any processing houses geared up to handle colour roll film. Also, developing was a long and complicated process. It would be some years before these films increased sufficiently in speed and ease of use for colour railway photographs to appear in any numbers.

All of the author's own photographs in this book were taken with permits obtained from George Dow, the LNER (later Eastern Region) Press & Public Relations Officer. He was very helpful, as were all the railway staff encountered during the photographic sorties, who were always willing to be of assistance, albeit sometimes with a degree of amused tolerance.

Below: In the first year of Nationalisation five-month-old 'A2' Pacific No 525 *A. H. Peppercorn*, still in its LNER guise, leaves King's Cross with the 6.5pm Leeds train on 11 May 1948. On the extreme left a train for the 'Widened Lines' stands at the York Road platform. *E. R. Wethersett*

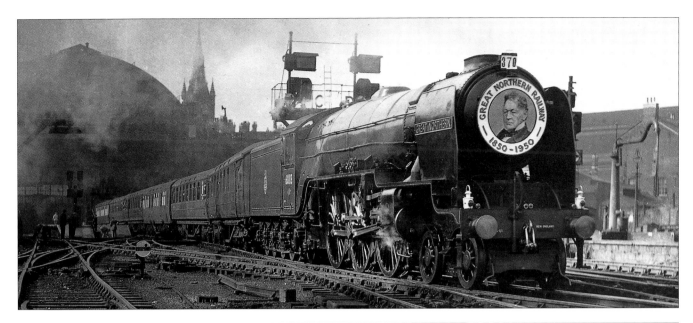

Above: Two years later the centenary of the GNR's arrival in London — at Maiden Lane, two years before King's Cross station opened — was marked by a special train to York. The first Chairman of the GNR, Michael Denison, graces the headboard as 'A1' No 60113 *Great Northern* leaves the terminus on 16 July 1950. Built in 1922 as GNR No 1470, this locomotive was Gresley's first Pacific; later LNER No 4470, it was controversially 'rebuilt' by Thompson in 1945 as the prototype for a new 'A1' class. *E. R. Wethersett*

Right: Emerging from Copenhagen Tunnel and passing Copenhagen Junction (both named after an ancient tavern that used to stand nearby) on the approach to King's Cross on a sunny 7 July 1947 is 'A4' No 6 *Sir Ralph Wedgwood*. This was the second 'A4' to carry the name, the first having been damaged beyond repair in an air raid on York in June 1942; No 6 was formerly *Herring Gull*. The end of the cul-de-sac of Frederick Street, above the tunnel, was later the location for Mrs Wilberforce's house in the classic 1955 Ealing comedy *The Ladykillers*, and much of the murderous action of the film took place above the portals! *E. R. Wethersett*

Right: A little further north a pair of 'N2' 0-6-2 tanks, Nos 9533 and 9505, pass Holloway — not, as the destination board would indicate, with a local for Hertford but with the empty stock of the 'Flying Scotsman' — on 27 May 1947. The leading locomotive still has its condensing pipes, designed to reduce emissions on the underground 'Widened Lines' between King's Cross and Moorgate. *E. R. Wethersett*

Right: A push-pull service operated between Finsbury Park on the main line and Alexandra Palace via Highgate. On 29 June 1946 2-4-2T No 5783 sets off for the branch.
E. R. Wethersett

Below: In early 1947, after running for only three months, the 'Yorkshire Pullman' was withdrawn due to a fuel crisis brought on by a period of very severe weather. It returned in October, and is seen here on the 6th behind 'A3' 4-6-2 No 104 *Solario*, in apple-green livery, on the up fast line passing Wood Green Tunnel down signalbox. *E. R. Wethersett*

Right: No 61619 *Welbeck Abbey*, one of Gresley's Class B17/1 'Sandringham' 4-6-0s, formerly No 2819. Built from 1928, the class was originally used on the Great Eastern line, including the Harwich boat trains, and later on the former Great Central, but on 30 August 1948 this locomotive — with BR number but 'L N E R' on the tender — was working on the East Coast main line, being seen passing New Southgate with a down stopping train. A further batch built at Darlington in 1936 were named after well-known football clubs, beginning with No 2848 *Arsenal*.
E. R.Wethersett

Right: The first 'A4' to carry the name *Woodcock*, No 4489, became *Dominion of Canada* a couple of months later for the introduction of the 'Coronation' streamliner, whereupon No 4493 assumed the earlier name. In the LNER's 1946 renumbering scheme this locomotive became No 29, being seen here with a down express at New Southgate on 5 July 1947. Following Nationalisation BR would add 60,000 to the LNER number, *Woodcock* becoming No 60029. *E. R. Wethersett*

Above: Just over two years old, 'B1' 4-6-0 No 1005 *Bongo* passes New Southgate with a down Cambridge train on 20 April 1946. The 'B1s' carried the names of antelopes, the first being named *Springbok* in honour of a visit to the UK by General Smuts, the wartime South African leader. Management encouraged the use of 'Antelope' class to describe them; however, once No 1005 had arrived, among railwaymen they were thereafter 'Bongos'! *E. R. Wethersett*

Right: This 'V2' 2-6-2 was also photographed at New Southgate, on 9 April 1949, by which time it was carrying its BR number (60922) and 'BRITISH RAILWAYS' in full on the tender. It is hauling a down express of decidedly mixed vehicles. *E. R. Wethersett*

Left: At the head of a goods train at New Southgate is former 'K4' 2-6-0 No 3445 *MacCailin Mor*. The name *MacCailein Mor* was originally applied to No 3442, but within a fortnight the mis-spelling had been noticed and the name replaced by *The Great Marquess*, now preserved. No 3445 received the correctly spelled nameplate in 1939, then in 1945 was rebuilt by Thompson as the prototype 'K1', in which form it is seen here on 23 April 1946; later in the year it would be renumbered 1997. Upon Nationalisation it would become No 61997, the production locomotives, refined by Peppercorn, arriving as Nos 62001-70 in 1949/50. *E. R. Wethersett*

Right: A fine view of the purposeful profile of the first 'A1', No 60114, seen heading a down express at New Southgate just after entering traffic in August 1948. It would have its *W. P. Allen* nameplates added later that month. This was the month when extensive flooding breached the East Coast line north of Berwick, and trains were diverted via Kelso and Galashiels; the non-stop services thus ran for almost 410 miles, over a harder route and with one fewer set of water troughs.
E. R. Wethersett

Left: The non-stop King's Cross–Edinburgh 'Capitals Limited' was launched by actress Anne Crawford on 23 May 1949.
On 8 September 1951 the down train passes Potters Bar behind 'A4' No 60025 *Falcon*; the train became the 'Elizabethan' in 1953. Heading south with a train from Cambridge is Class B17/4 'Footballer' 4-6-0 No 61652 *Darlington*; note the nameplate, with a brass football flanked by stripes painted in the club's colours. Although additional up and down lines are evident here, there were serious double-track bottlenecks through the stations and tunnels between New Barnet and Potters Bar until the line was quadrupled in the years 1953-9, a scheme first proposed by the LNER in 1946. *E. R. Wethersett*

Right: Controlling the reduction in tracks from four to two at the north end of the section was Woolmer Green signalbox, seen in the distance of this 16 May 1952 view of 'V2' No 60909 heading towards Welwyn North Tunnel with an up express. The line over Welwyn Viaduct and through Welwyn North station and Welwyn Tunnels remains a two-track bottleneck to this day. *E. R. Wethersett*

Right: Stevenage saw the beginning of huge development when it became the first New Town to be so designated under the terms of the 1946 New Towns Act, to accommodate postwar population overspill. Two years later, on 3 July 1948, 'A3' Pacific No 108 (soon to become No 60108) *Gay Crusader* passes with a down fast goods. *E. R. Wethersett*

Right: Hitchin station lies in a chalk cutting, as can be seen in this view of veteran 'J3' 0-6-0 No 4122, a Gresley larger-boilered rebuild of the earlier Stirling and Ivatt 'J4'. The first of the class to be withdrawn was Hitchin's No 4145, on 2 March 1948; No 4122, also a Hitchin resident, was photographed on 3 July of that year. All had gone by 1954. *E. R. Wethersett*

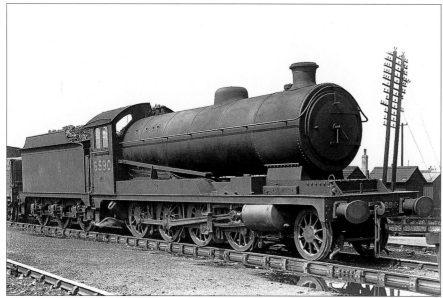

Above: Peterborough station was another notorious bottleneck on the East Coast main line, necessitating speed restrictions until the tracks were realigned and the station rebuilt in the 1970s. North of Peterborough the Spalding line swung northeastwards at Werrington Junction, then followed Werrington water troughs. Heading north over the troughs on 26 April 1951 is the 2pm King's Cross–Edinburgh express headed by 'A1' No 60135 *Madge Wildfire*, one of several of the Peppercorn Pacifics named after characters in Sir Walter Scott's novels (in this case *Heart of Midlothian*). On the extreme right can be seen the parallel ex-Midland Railway route, which soon departs westward towards Stamford. *E. R. Wethersett*

Centre left: The Robinson 'O4' 2-8-0s were built by the Great Central Railway and were thus inherited by the LNER. Between 1944 and 1958 some 99 locomotives were rebuilt with Thompson 'B1' boilers and side-window cabs to become Class O4/8, one of which, No 6590, was photographed at Peterborough on 2 June 1946. *E. R. Wethersett*

Left: The famous Stoke Bank, scene of *Mallard*'s 1938 triumph, comprised 5 miles at 1 in 200. Coasting down the grade from Stoke Tunnel is another of the 'Walter Scott' Class A1 Pacifics, No 60124 *Kenilworth*, with the up 'Northumbrian' on 30 July 1951. *E. R. Wethersett*

Right: The name of the designer of the 'A2/3' Pacifics, *Edward Thompson*, was applied to the first of the class, No 60500, in 1946, the year he retired. The last locomotive built during his term of office, it is seen here at the summit of Stoke Bank at the head of a down Newcastle express on 30 July 1951. *E. R. Wethersett*

Centre right: The 'A5' 4-6-2 tank was another GCR design absorbed by the LNER at the Grouping. One of the 1911 originals, No 9817, is seen at its home shed, Grantham, on 12 July 1948. Modifications to later examples were made in 1925, but all of these had been scrapped by the end of the 1950s, while four of the originals survived into the early 1960s in Lincolnshire. *E. R. Wethersett*

Below left: Dukeries Junction, between Newark and Retford, was where the grandly titled Lancashire, Derbyshire & East Coast Railway, taken over by the GCR in 1907, crossed the East Coast main line, and there were platforms at both levels. This photograph was taken from the signalbox and shows an express from King's Cross to Newcastle during the summer of 1949. Motive power is provided by 'A4' No 60017 *Silver Fox*, one of the original 'Silver Jubilee' streamliners. This was the locomotive used in May 1946 on trial runs between King's Cross and Edinburgh to test the track condition at high speeds, and on the up journey a speed of 102mph was reached between Grantham and Peterborough. However, the results were not encouraging, as the speed limits in force at the time were not relaxed. *John Dove*

Below right: A 'V2' 2-6-2 mixed-traffic locomotive, No 60954, passes the same spot with a northbound relief express in August 1949. *John Dove*

Above left: No 60511 *Airborne* was the second of Thompson's 'A2/3s' to be built from scratch, earlier examples being rebuilds of Gresley locomotives. Here, on 11 September 1949, it thunders past Dukeries Junction signalbox at the head of an express from King's Cross. *John Dove*

Above: The author's father has a grandstand view from Dukeries Junction 'box on 11 September 1949 as Peppercorn 'A1' No 60125, as yet unnamed, passes with a southbound express. All the staff were very welcoming, and an enjoyable afternoon was spent taking photographs in and around this location. *John Dove*

Left: Peppercorn 'A1' No 60131, also not yet named, heads south through Dukeries Junction station with an express from Leeds in August 1949. *John Dove*

Left: 'A4' No 60020 *Guillemot*, at the head of an express from Newcastle, passes under the old Great Central line between Chesterfield and Lincoln in August 1949. The porter standing on the overbridge was one of the very few staff remaining at this station; something of a failure as an interchange point, it would close seven months after this photograph was taken, on 6 March 1950. *John Dove*

Right: Dukeries Junction can be seen in the distance as an express for Edinburgh passes Tuxford Junction 'box during the summer of 1949 headed by a Gresley 'A4'. The line to the right linked with the ex-GC line at Tuxford Central and was used for freight traffic exchange until closure in 1964. *John Dove*

Right: With steam to spare, Class A3 No 60047 *Donovan* heads a down express approaching Tuxford Junction in August 1949. *John Dove*

Below: An unidentified 'V2' photographed between Dukeries Junction and Tuxford at the head of a down express during August 1949. This was coal-mining country, as evidenced by the large number of empty coal wagons in the sidings. *John Dove*

Left: Peppercorn 'A2' No E527 *Sun Chariot* heads south past Tuxford North station in early BR days. The modern concrete-post signal controls the junction with the spur to the GC line.

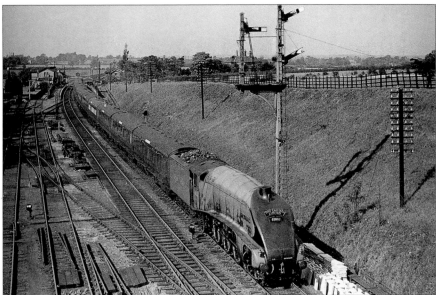

Left: It is the summer of 1949, and the up 'Capitals Limited' is heading through the Nottinghamshire countryside behind No 60011 *Empire of India*. This was a Haymarket 'A4' and was normally seen this far south only on the non-stop 'Capitals Limited'. The train has just passed Tuxford North station, which was closed in 1955. *John Dove*

Below left: Markham signalbox was located on the climb to Askham Tunnel, north of Tuxford, where the down loop ended. A local goods train waits in the loop for a northbound express to pass, headed by 'A3' Pacific No 60059 *Tracery*. *John Dove*

Below: Another 'A3', No 60085 *Manna*, passes the same train of empty coal wagons waiting to join the fast line at Markham. *John Dove*

Above: Viewed from the opposite direction, a Class V2 heads south with a Saturday relief passenger train on 23 July 1949. It has just breasted Markham Summit, having threaded the short Askham Tunnel.

Above right: On the same day the up 'Flying Scotsman' was headed by No 60019 *Bittern*, one of the six preserved Gresley 'A4s', withdrawn after 30 years of illustrious service in 1966. The colour-light signal was a recent replacement for a semaphore type. Signals remote from signalboxes were among the first to be changed owing to the difficulties inherent in mechanical operation over long distances.

Right: Another up express passes Askham Summit behind Class A1 No 60142.
John Dove

Right: Class A4 No 60010 *Dominion of Canada* heads an express from Edinburgh past the same spot. The bell mounted on the smokebox was presented by the Canadian Pacific Railway, together with a Canadian chime whistle, which had the typical mournful North American sound — a note deeper than that of the other 'A4s'. This locomotive would be shipped to Canada after withdrawal from service and is now to be found at the Canadian Railway Museum in Montreal.

Above: An express from Leeds and Bradford headed by 'A2' Pacific No 60500 *Edward Thompson*, the 2,000th locomotive to be built at Doncaster, passes Askham Summit in April 1951. Appointed following the untimely death of Sir Nigel Gresley, Thompson was the controversial Chief Mechanical Engineer of the LNER from 1941 to 1946. His 'A2s' continued to be built until August 1947, when they were superseded by Peppercorn's development of the class.

Left: The 'Queen of Scots' Pullman leaves Askham Tunnel on its way to King's Cross during the summer of 1949. It is headed by Class A1 Pacific No 60139, shortly to be named *Sea Eagle* — a name originally carried by a Gresley 'A4'. Although new, more elegant smokebox headboards were now available (see page 6) No 60139 is still carrying the old prewar type.

Left: One of the 'Austerities' purchased by the LNER from the War Department at the end of 1946 and classified 'O7', No 90103 (previously LNER No 77003) is seen in early 1951 at the head of a heavy goods train emerging from the short Askham Tunnel. This was close to coal-mining country, as evidenced by three of the wagons on the train being loaded with pit-props.

Right: Gresley Class A3 No 53 *Sansovino* emerges from Askham Tunnel with an express for King's Cross in the summer of 1948. This locomotive was built as one of the earlier Gresley 'A1' Pacifics, entering service in 1924 and rebuilt as an 'A3' in 1943.

Right: Gateshead-based 'A4' No 18 *Sparrow Hawk* leaves the Askham Tunnel with an express from Newcastle, also during the summer of 1948. The locomotive has the raised stainless-steel numbers and tender lettering first used in 1937 on the 'A4s' allocated to the 'Coronation' streamlined express.

Below: The typical syncopated beat of a Gresley Pacific can readily be imagined in this photograph of No 15 *Quicksilver* pounding up the final 1-in-200 ascent to Markham Summit with an express from Newcastle on the afternoon of 20 November 1948. This 'A4' was one of the original batch of four built in 1935.

Left: North of Askham Tunnel, on the descent towards Retford, the Gamston signalman sends 'Train Entering Section' to Retford South signalbox as a King's Cross–Newcastle / Glasgow express passes. The locomotive, with its smokebox in deep shadow in this against-the-light photograph in the low winter sun of late December 1948, is Peppercorn 'A2' No 60535 *Hornets Beauty*.

Below: The inaugural up 'Tees–Tyne Pullman' of 27 September 1948 climbs past Gamston towards Askham Tunnel and Markham Summit from the north, hauled by Peppercorn 'A1' No 60115, then only a month old.

Left: Passing the same spot on 28 March 1950 is a southbound express from Leeds, Harrogate and Hull, with Gresley 'A4' Pacific No 60026 *Miles Beevor* in charge. The train is 2 miles south of Retford, which it would have left at 2.15pm.

Right: Class A1 Pacific No 60132 *Marmion* seems to be making light work of the 1-in-178 climb to Markham Summit with the up 'Flying Scotsman' on the afternoon of 28 March 1951.

Right: Seen at the same spot on the same afternoon, Class V2 2-6-2 No 60966 is producing rather more exhaust at the head of a relief express for King's Cross.

Below: 'Distant at clear'. The 11.15am express from Edinburgh is promised a clear road past Gamston 'box as it heads south up the incline to the summit at Markham on its way to King's Cross behind 'A4' No 60021 *Golden Plover*, happily still bearing its original name. The date is 31 July 1949.

Above: This Class A4 Pacific has been drafted in for a task normally undertaken at that time by an Ivatt Atlantic — the local passenger train from Doncaster to Newark. On a glorious sunny afternoon in late July 1949, No 60021 *Wild Swan* is seen ambling up Gamston Bank at Eaton Wood with the 5.30pm ex Retford.

Left: At the same location three days later, Monday 1 August, in very different dull and wet weather conditions, Class C1 Ivatt Atlantic No 2839 is seen working harder with the evening train, which was due out of Retford at 7.23pm. The exposure variations are interesting. The above photograph was taken at 1/900th of a second at f6.3 and this one required 1/450th of a second at f3.5.

Above: To many railway enthusiasts this may seem like an idyllic scene long since disappeared — no forest of posts holding up catenaries and a mass of other wires, no pre-stressed concrete structures, just wonky telegraph poles and an old iron-and-brick bridge. The camera had been set up on the evening of 10 August 1950 for the southbound 'Queen of Scots', due along in a few minutes, when pottering up the slow line came 'A4' *William Whitelaw*, just out of Doncaster Plant in the short-lived BR blue livery after major overhaul. The name was originally carried by an 'A3' but was transferred to this 'A4' in July 1941. It seems surprising that, with the London Blitz barely over (King's Cross and Liverpool Street stations having been badly damaged in an air raid only two months previously), the LNER had the time, resources or inclination to fiddle about changing locomotive names.

Right: 'The Queen of Scots' duly appeared behind Class A1 No 60119 *Patrick Stirling*.

Above: On a blustery winter's day, 20 January 1949, the southbound 'Yorkshire Pullman' headed by No 60119 passes Eaton Wood. No 60119 was almost new when this photograph was taken, having been completed at Doncaster Plant in November 1948.

Left: Seen from the other side of the line, Class A3 No 63 *Isinglass* is also on the 4-mile climb to Askham, passing beneath Eaton Wood bridge, in November 1948; almost a year after Nationalisation the locomotive still carries its LNER number and tender lettering. The train is the morning express from Ripon, Harrogate and Hull.

Right: Photographed on 19 January 1949, No 60049 *Galtee More* was built as Gresley Class A1 No 2548 in 1924; subsequently rebuilt as an 'A3', it became No 49 under the LNER renumbering of 1946. The train is a Leeds/Bradford–King's Cross express, seen storming under Eaton Wood bridge, having left Retford 5 minutes previously. The bridge was the original structure built by the Great Northern Railway *c*1850, of riveted steel construction and designed for light road usage only. It would be replaced during the electrification of the East Coast main line, as would many other bridges, owing to a lack of headroom for the overhead catenary.

Right: Approaching the bridge from the north, 'A3' No 60049 *Galtee More* climbs Gamston Bank with an express from Hull. It is late November 1948, and the cast British Railways smokebox numberplates are becoming more commonplace.

Right: Class A3 Pacific No E62 *Minoru* passes the same spot on its way from Leeds and Bradford to King's Cross on the morning of 19 January 1949. The post-Nationalisation 'E' prefix was used in only a relatively few instances, most locomotives waiting for their official BR numbers, whereby 60,000 would be added to the LNER numbers (*Minoru* thus becoming No 60062).

Above: Back on the down side of the line, the author's camera was set to take a photograph of the down 'Flying Scotsman' as this up express from Edinburgh passed Eaton Wood in the early afternoon of 5 January 1949. Motive power was provided by Thompson 'A2' No 60512 *Steady Aim. John Dove*

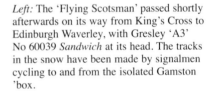

Left: The 'Flying Scotsman' passed shortly afterwards on its way from King's Cross to Edinburgh Waverley, with Gresley 'A3' No 60039 *Sandwich* at its head. The tracks in the snow have been made by signalmen cycling to and from the isolated Gamston 'box.

Left: In much more clement weather, on the evening of 28 July 1949, Class V2 No 60855 passes beneath the bridge on its way north with a relief express passenger train.

Right: With Eaton Wood bridge in the distance, this is the view from the first carriage of a southbound Leeds–King's Cross express as it climbs Gamston Bank behind an 'A4' Pacific. *John Dove*

Right: Thompson 'A2/3' Pacific No 60521 *Watling Street* hard at work and making much smoke as it gets away from Retford past Grove Road level crossing on 21 March 1951. The train is an express from Ripon, Harrogate and Bradford to King's Cross, scheduled to call at Retford at 12.52pm every weekday. Many of Thompson's 'A2s' suffered from the steam leakage shown here, which was caused by the escape of steam from an expansion joint in the exhaust system; the joint was necessary to prevent breakage in the tube to the blastpipe, which had to be much longer than was usual because of the chosen outside cylinder position.

Below: Gresley 'A4' No 3 *Andrew K. McCosh* in full cry at the head of the up 'Yorkshire Pullman' passing Grove Road in the spring of 1948. This was where the up slow line for the climb of Gamston Bank began. The locomotive was originally *Osprey*, being renamed in late 1942.

Above: Headed by Peppercorn 'A1'
No 60128, the 7.50am express from Leeds
to King's Cross passes under London Road
bridge at Ordsall, just outside Retford.
This was one of the services used for the 1948
Locomotive Exchanges; at that time unnamed,
it became the 'West Riding' in the 1949
summer timetable, effective about two months
before this photograph was taken.

Left: In a very wintry scene in January 1949
No 22 *Mallard*, at the head of an express from
Edinburgh, can be seen sporting the plaque
fitted in 1948 to commemorate the breaking
of the world record for steam traction some
10 years earlier. Comparison with the
previoius picture will reveal that the stop arm
has been removed from the signal. *John Dove*

Above: Accelerating away from its stop at Retford, a southbound express headed by 'A1' Pacific No 60144 prepares to attack Gamston Bank.

Right: One of the numerous Ivatt Class J6 0-6-0s, No 64263, approaches Grove at the head of a southbound local mixed goods on 31 December 1948.

Above: A 'V2' on a fast northbound freight approaches Retford on a cold January day in 1949. *John Dove*

Left: Thompson 'A2/3' Pacific No 522 *Straight Deal* enters the 65mph speed limit for the level crossing of the East Coast main line and the ex-Great Central Lincoln–Sheffield line just south of Retford station on Christmas Eve 1948. The train is a morning express from King's Cross to Newcastle, Glasgow and Aberdeen.

Left: Class A3 No 60048 *Doncaster* pulls away from Retford at the head of the 11.47am express from Harrogate and Hull to King's Cross on 4 December 1948. The 'A3s' managed to avoid the wholesale renaming suffered by the 'A4s' and were nearly all named after racehorses that had won the Derby or St Leger. Among the exceptions were *Great Northern*, *Flying Scotsman*, *Centenary* (to celebrate 100 years of Doncaster Plant), *Dick Turpin*, *William Whitelaw* (transferred to an 'A4' in 1941, the 'A3' being renamed *Tagalie*) and *Knight of Thistle*. The locomotive featured here might be imagined to fall into this category but in fact was named after a horse that won the Derby in 1873.

Above: It is mid-day on 31 December 1948, and the sun has just broken through, only half an hour after the end of a heavy snowstorm. Having cleared the Retford Crossing speed restriction, 'A1' Pacific No 60116 picks up speed to attack Gamston Bank with the southbound 'Tees–Tyne Pullman'. This locomotive entered service from Doncaster Works in October of that year and later became *Hal o' the Wynd* — an evocative and appropriate name for a Peppercorn 'A1'. This photograph was featured on the 1950 Christmas card of the Hunslet Engine Co Ltd, Leeds, one of the last independent manufacturers of steam locomotives to survive in this country.

Right: Carrying its temporary BR number, E62, Class A3 *Minoru* is seen leaving Retford with an express from Leeds. The date is 4 December 1948.

Above: The up 'Tees–Tyne Pullman' sweeps through Retford on its way south on 27 October 1948. Having brought the train from Newcastle, the crew will be looking forward to their changeover at Grantham, about 30 miles away. Locomotive No 60115 was the second Peppercorn 'A1' to be built and would shortly be named *Meg Merrilies*.

Left: Class K2/1 No 61723 in charge of a mixed freight passing Retford. This locomotive, one of a class of only 10, was a 1931 rebuild of a 'K1', built some 20 years earlier. These locomotives, together with the 'K2/2s', were a common sight at the head of goods trains in the Eastern Counties.

Right: Photographed in 1950, the 'Yorkshire Pullman' has just passed through Retford station on its way to King's Cross; the motive power is provided by Peppercorn 'A1' No 60134.

Below: Another Peppercorn 'A1', No 60136, at the head of a Leeds express, pulling away from its stop at Retford with the 11.32am for King's Cross on a cold January day in 1949. The rail level crossing was in front of Retford South signalbox, and the wooden fencing of the sharply curved GC-line platform can be seen on the extreme right.

Right: Retford-based Class B1 No 61212 waits for the road south of Retford station with a local train. *John Dove*

Above left: This dramatic shot was taken in 1950 from the coach of a train just leaving Retford station for King's Cross as the 'Tees–Tyne Pullman' thundered past. On the right are 'J39' No 64835, one of the freight workhorses of the Eastern Region, and No 61727, a Class K2 mixed-traffic locomotive. *John Dove*

Above right: It is April 1949, and Peppercorn 'A1' No 60125, having just been completed at Doncaster Plant, is gleaming in its LNER apple-green livery on its running-in turn to Barkston Junction triangle, just north of Grantham. Barkston was a much-used junction for turning locomotives; it was here that *Mallard* and its dynamometer car were turned in preparation for the record-breaking run of 1938. *John Dove*

Centre left: The 'B17' 4-6-0s were introduced in 1928 and were intended primarily for use on the Great Eastern section of the LNER; all but two of the original batch of 48 were named after stately homes and known as 'Sandringhams'. Unusually for a new project, they were designed by an outside contractor, the North British Locomotive Co Ltd of Glasgow, which also built the first 10. A second batch, numbering 25, was built in 1936/7 by Robert Stephenson & Co in Darlington and by the LNER's own Darlington Works; these were named after leading football teams of the day and were initially used on the Great Central line out of Marylebone. Here, on 12 January 1949, No E1667 *Bradford* stands in Retford station with the 2.55pm train for Cleethorpes; Retford was an interchange station for the East Coast main line and the Great Central line between Sheffield and the East Coast.

Left: Immingham-based Robinson Class D11 'Enlarged Director' 4-4-0 No 62665 *Mons* pulls out of Retford station with an eastbound local stopping train on 24 December 1949.

Above: At mid-day on 24 December 1949 an express from Sheffield leaves Retford *en route* for Gainsborough, Immingham and Grimsby. Motive power is supplied by Ivatt Atlantic No 62885, one of a class of locomotives that 25 years earlier would have more usually been seen at the head of East Coast expresses. They continued to distinguish themselves long after the introduction of Gresley's Pacifics, notably on the 'Queen of Scots', 'Yorkshire Pullman' and other West Riding expresses.

Right: A Class K3 2-6-0 at the head of a westbound freight train on the Great Central line approaches the level crossing with the East Coast main line at Retford. *John Dove*

Left: Seen on the ex-Great Central line is one of Robinson's original 'Director' 4-4-0s, built in 1913. Class D10 No 2657 *Sir Berkeley Sheffield*, appropriately based at Sheffield motive-power depot, is here seen on an express from Cleethorpes to Sheffield, next stop Worksop.

Left: A coal train from Manton Colliery, a few miles down the line at Worksop, heads towards the East Coast main line, with about two miles to go. Motive power is provided by Class J11 0-6-0 No 64380, one of a class of 174 locomotives built by the GCR and various contractors in the years 1901-10. *John Dove*

Left: Photographed on 21 December 1949, one of Robinson's handsome Class D11 'Enlarged Director' 4-4-0s makes a spirited start from Retford, heading along the chord from Retford North Junction to Whisker Hill Junction on the GC route towards its next stop, Worksop, with the morning express from Cleethorpes to Sheffield. The 'D11s' were introduced in 1920 and continued to be produced after the Grouping of 1923, finally numbering some 35 locomotives. Seen here is No 62666 *Zeebrugge*, which would be withdrawn in 1960, the last example following only a year later.

Right: Class B1 4-6-0 No 61281 rounds the curve from Retford station to join up with the Lincoln–Sheffield line. *John Dove*

Left: A December 1948 photograph showing Retford station from the north-west. In the foreground is the line from Whisker Hill Junction. *John Dove*

Right: The 'Austerities' had few faults, but one was that the tender's front wheels were prone to derailing on sharp curves. On the evening of 5 October 1947 2-8-0 No 70834, on the right, finds itself in just such a predicament on the Great Central curve by Retford North signalbox. Another 'Austerity' has brought the incident train, complete with crane, from Doncaster, while in the background can be seen a pair of locally based 'B1' 4-6-0s, Nos 1208 and 1212. The odd-looking steam effect is an indication of the time exposure necessary at this late hour.

Above: Class A4 No 60026 *Miles Beevor*, seen at the Great Northern shed at Retford, has only recently had its name changed from *Kestrel*. It is waiting to be towed to Doncaster, having failed on a southbound express. *John Dove*

Left: Re-laying track the old-fashioned way: renewal of the main line north of Retford station on Sunday 7 September 1947, which seems to require an awful lot of workers.

Below: At almost the same spot a few weeks later, on 5 October, the LNER's most famous locomotive, *Flying Scotsman*, finds itself in an ignominious position: having become derailed just north of the station, it awaits the arrival of the Doncaster-based steam crane.

Right: Photographed from an overbridge just north of Retford station just after the start of a heavy snowfall in January 1949, an express to Hull has just pulled out of the station to be met by a southbound fast fitted freight headed by a Gresley 'V2'. *John Dove*

Right: An up parcels train approaches Retford station headed by a very clean 'A4', No 15 *Quicksilver*, the second of the class to be built.

Below: Another of the original quartet of 'A4s', No 60016 *Silver King*, sounds a warning as it approaches Retford station with the up 'Flying Scotsman' on 25 September 1948.

Above: This was the view looking north from the footbridge seen in the previous photographs at dusk on 10 January 1949, showing the East Coast main line dead straight and rising on a 1-in-440 incline. The exposure time of 2min 45sec at f8 gives an indication of the film speeds available at the time. *John Dove*

Below: It is late October 1948, and 'A1' No 60117, the fourth locomotive of the class to be built, is only a few days old. It is being run in on the afternoon local passenger train and is on its way back to Doncaster.

Above: Headed by Peppercorn 'A2' No 60537 *Bachelors Button*, turned out by Doncaster a few months previously, the up 'Yorkshire Pullman' approaches Retford in the early autumn of 1948.

Right: Seen from the road bridge, No 16 *Silver King* heads south with the 'Flying Scotsman' in the summer of 1948.

Below: Late in the autumn of 1947 Class A3 No 46 *Diamond Jubilee* approaches Retford at the head of the up 'Yorkshire Pullman'. Turned out in 1924 as one of Gresley's early 'A1s', it was rebuilt as an 'A3' in 1941.

Above: Severe blizzard conditions were experienced at Retford during the winter of 1947/8; here the 'Yorkshire Pullman' approaches Retford behind 'A4' No 26 *Miles Beevor*, sporting yet another headboard variation.

Left: More blizzard conditions as 'V2' No 852 heads south with an express from Hull and Harrogate in December 1948. The photograph was taken from the lee side of Babworth Road bridge, which gave some protection to the camera (and the photographer!).

Above: Lacking its *Wild Swan* nameplates, Class A4 No 60021, heading south with a train of armoured vehicles, has obviously been pressed into service at short notice. *John Dove*

Right: Peppercorn Class A1 No 60124 speeds down the 1-in-440 gradient towards Retford station at the head of the southbound 'Flying Scotsman'. In the distance can be seen Canal signalbox.

Right: Peppercorn's first 'A1', No 60114 *W. P. Allen*, heads north with an express for Leeds and Bradford in December 1948. This locomotive was named after Bill Allen, an ex-Great Northern driver and General Secretary of ASLEF from 1940 to 1947. In October of the latter year, as Union representative, he became a member of the Railway Executive, which was then being formed to run the Nationalised British Railways.

Left: Class A3 No 60069 *Sceptre* at the head of an express for Edinburgh as it crosses the Chesterfield Canal in the summer of 1949. A hundred years previously the owners of this canal had vehemently opposed the building of the 'Towns Line', as this section of the East Coast main line was known. They had very good reason, as it turned out, most of their business being lost to the railway within a few years. *John Dove*

Above: The up 'Yorkshire Pullman' crosses the canal on 9 August 1950 with one of Peppercorn's 'A1s' in charge, No 60117 *Bois Roussel*. The locomotive has recently been fitted with the new British Railways standardised shedcode plate, based on that originated by the LMS, as seen on the smokebox door; this replaced the LNER practice of painting the shed name on the buffer-beam. At the same time British Railways gave all motive-power depots a code based on the LMS system: 37B on *Bois Roussel*'s plate indicates Copley Hill, Leeds.

Left: It was occasionally possible to use the weather as an excuse for being chauffeured to the lineside. A gathering storm is the backdrop to Gresley Class V2 No 811 as it speeds south past Canal signalbox with the 9.35am Sundays-only express from Glasgow to King's Cross on 2 May 1948.

Above: The 'Flying Scotsman' express was reinstated as a non-stop service between King's Cross and Edinburgh in the May 1948 timetable, but the non-stop run lasted only until the introduction of the 'Capitals Limited' a year later. Here we see No 60009 *Union of South Africa* speeding through the north Nottinghamshire countryside beyond Canal signalbox on 6 June 1948 with the down 'Flying Scotsman'. No 60009 was the last steam locomotive to be given a general overhaul at Doncaster; one of six preserved 'A4s', it occasionally graces the metals of the East Coast main line at the head of chartered steam specials.

Right: Thompson 'B1' 4-6-0 No 61213 heads a local stopping train near Retford. *John Dove*

Left: In a wintry scene on New Year's Day 1949 near Barnby Moor & Sutton, in Nottinghamshire, an express from King's Cross heads for Newcastle behind Gresley 'A4' No 60016 *Silver King*.

Left: On the same day the up 'Yorkshire Pullman' headed by Class A1 No 60136 (later named *Alcazar*) emerges from the North Road bridge at Barnby Moor. Some of the 'A1s' were built at Doncaster Plant, the remainder, including this locomotive, at Darlington. Thompson's four 'A2/1s' aside, this was the first time that Pacifics had been built at the old North Eastern Railway's works since Raven's quintet of the 1920s.

Right: 'A4' Pacific No 60008 about to pass under the North Road bridge with the down 'Flying Scotsman' on a cold winter's day in January 1949. This locomotive, built in 1937, was originally No 4496 *Golden Shuttle* and allocated for use on the 'West Riding Limited'. The first 'A4' to be repainted Garter blue after the war, in September 1945, it was at that time renamed *Dwight D. Eisenhower* to honour the Allies' Supreme Commander during World War 2, who had an association with the LNER in that it had specially armoured and modified a coach for his use in Europe after the D-Day landings. The locomotive is now in the American National Railway Museum at Green Bay, Wisconsin.

Right: The location of this spring 1951 photograph is Pipers Wood, Bawtry, near Doncaster. Passing with a southbound express, Class A3 No 60073 *St Gatien* was then allocated to Heaton depot, where a team of dedicated cleaners managed to keep their locomotives much cleaner than those of many sheds.

Centre right: A Gresley 'A3' at the head of an up express feels its way southward in a thick late-autumn fog. It is just about to cross the River Idle near Bawtry, considerably slower than the indicated 70mph speed limit, which in these conditions is purely academic. The date is 27 November 1948.

Below left: Still bearing its old number at Doncaster on 1 September 1946 is Class O2 2-8-0 No 3465 of Frodingham shed. Known originally as the 'O1' class but reclassified by Thompson, 20 of these Gresley-designed locomotives were built for the GNR in the years 1913-19. *E. R. Wethersett*

Below right: Photographed at Doncaster on the same day was 'Q1' 0-8-0T No 9936, a 1943 Thompson rebuild of a Robinson GCR Class 8A of 1902 (LNER Class Q4). Note the LNER 'totem' plate on the bunker side; this was one of the few applications of this emblem on locomotives, originally it had raised white letters on a blue background. *E. R. Wethersett*

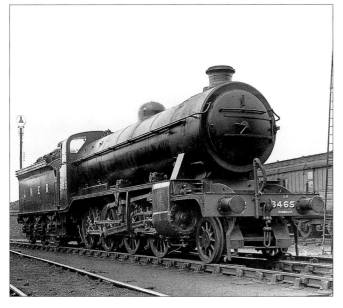

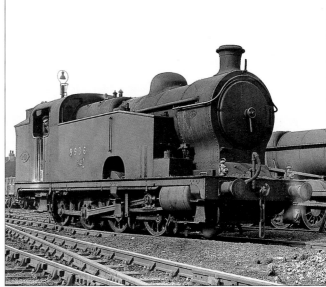

Above: Opened in 1853, the famous Doncaster Works, known as The Plant, eventually covered 84 acres and employed 3,000 men on 600 machines. Seen on 17 July 1948 in a sorry state, having lost its wheels and boiler in the early stages of a major overhaul, is Class B1 4-6-0 No 1098.

Above right: 'How are the mighty fallen': a couple of withdrawn Ivatt Atlantics adapted as stationary boilers for the Works.

Below: Chaloners Whin, 2 miles south of York, was the junction of the Sheffield/Leeds line via Church Fenton and the East Coast main line from Selby, and the four tracks south from York station meant that trains for the two routes could be despatched separately — and occasionally together, leading to some racing! 'A3' Pacific No 60074 *Harvester* comes off the Selby line with a King's Cross–Edinburgh express on 16 August 1948. *E. R. Wethersett*

Above: Raven 'B16' 4-6-0 No 1441 heads an up express goods past Chaloners Whin Junction on 10 July 1948. Some of the signals on the gantry, notably the second and third from the left, still have NER slotted posts. *E. R. Wethersett*

Right: 'A3' No 60053 *Sansovino* heads south past Chaloners Whin signalbox on 5 August 1951 — note the 'York 2' milepost. This junction would cease to exist with the opening in 1983 of the Selby diversion. *E. R. Wethersett*

Left: The LNER Class C7 Atlantics were a Vincent Raven design for the North Eastern Railway, introduced in 1911. No 732 was built by the North British Locomotive Co and in 1933 was fitted with Lentz rotary-cam poppet valvegear. It is seen here at York shed on 7 September 1946, the year that it was allocated new LNER number 2963. Only 14 of the class would pass into BR ownership in 1948, none surviving beyond the end of that year. *E. R. Wethersett*

Left: Introduced in 1899, the elegant Wilson Worsdell NER Class R 4-4-0s became the LNER's Class D20, and a considerable number passed into BR ownership, the last survivor being withdrawn in 1959. No 2392, built in 1907, was allocated to Starbeck shed, Harrogate, when photographed at the north end of York station on 16 August 1948. *E. R. Wethersett*

Left: Another ex-NER Worsdell (LNER 'D20') 4-4-0, No 2391, leaves Northallerton station with a Stockton local on 26 August 1947. The train is passing the signalbox built in 1939 to house a modern interlocking route-setting signalling panel, as part of the LNER's modernisation of signalling on the East Coast main line. It was one of only three 'boxes that now controlled the 14 miles between Northallerton and Darlington, and the panel incorporated the very first use of white route-lights to indicate which route had been set, with 129 possible settings. In contrast the new panel designed for York had no fewer than 825 routes! *E. R. Wethersett*

Left: The LNER 'Q6' 0-8-0 was a Raven NER design ('6F') introduced in 1913. No 3454, with its shed allocation of West Hartlepool on the buffer-beam, approaches the water troughs at Wiske Moor, about two miles north of Northallerton, with a down goods on 26 August 1947. *E. R. Wethersett*

Left: This stretch of line had been the subject of earlier pioneering automatic-signalling schemes, in particular experimental gas-operated semaphore signals in 1905, which lasted until the advent of early colour-light signalling in 1933. One odd result of pneumatic signals is shown here, supposedly something that 'couldn't happen': distant signals were always interlocked so that they returned to 'danger' simultaneously with the stop signal, regardless of the position of the operating lever; in this instance the distant signal is operated by an electro-pneumatic valve, and the time taken for the air to be released from the valve is sufficient to allow the stop arm, mechanically operated by wire, to return to 'danger' first. *John Dove*

Right: Class A3 Pacific No 60083 *Sir Hugo*, at the head of a down express, takes water on the troughs on 6 August 1949.

Above: On the same day 'B1' 4-6-0 No E1289 heads an up relief passenger train, comprising a somewhat motley collection of coaches, past the south water tank at Wiske Moor. The troughs were fed from the River Wiske, which is close by at this point, and were shortly to be completely rebuilt.

Above: No 60042 *Singapore* passes the north water tank at Wiske Moor troughs at the head of an up Newcastle express in August 1949. Shortly after this photograph was taken the troughs had a major upgrade, having remained substantially unaltered since they were laid down at the beginning of the century. One major shortcoming was that the refill time after a train had passed was about 10 minutes, which could cause operational problems, so it was decided to replace both the troughs and rails and the replenishment system. A new design of trough was used with a turned-in top lip to reduce splashing, while the old bull-head rails were replaced by the new standard flat-bottomed type. The replenishment-system upgrade was a success, reducing the filling time to 2 minutes.

Left: The troughs and drainage arrangements are seen more clearly in this 26 August 1948 photograph of 'A4' No 16 *Silver King* heading south with the up 'Flying Scotsman'. *E. R. Wethersett*

Left: The driver of this unnamed Peppercorn Pacific keeps a wary eye on the track-maintenance gang as he heads for London with the 'Tees–Tyne Pullman' on the morning of 20 April 1949. The train is near Croft Spa aerodrome, some 4 miles south of Darlington, from where it was timetabled to make a non-stop run to King's Cross, although initially it called at Grantham to change footplate crews. That stop was abolished a month after this photograph was taken, with the introduction of the summer timetable, when it was agreed that the same crew should man the train throughout its journey between Newcastle and King's Cross. It then became an onerous turn of nearly 270 miles, especially for the fireman, who would be expected to fire upwards of 5 tons of coal. However, when there was a close rapport between the crew it was not uncommon for the driver to do short stints on the shovel to give his fireman a break.

Above: A trio of lengthmen carry on with their work unconcerned by passing Gresley Pacific No 60085 *Manna*, which is well into its stride after its stop at Darlington with a morning Newcastle–King's Cross express on 20 April 1949

Right: On the same day Class V2 No 60944 heads south away from Darlington with a relief express. This time the men have stopped work!

Right: An up semi-fast from Newcastle approaches Harrowgate Hill, north of Darlington, with Class B1 4-6-0 No 61021 *Reitbok* in charge. Eventually numbering 410 in total, locomotives of this class were still being built at the time of this photograph, April 1949. A total of 58 carried names, 40 of which were mainly obscure kinds of antelope. With names such as *Puku*, *Duiker*, *Madoqua*, *Dibatag* and *Jairou* they could well have been chosen to confound rail enthusiasts!

Left: Having just passed Harrowgate Hill, a very grubby 'V2' heads for Newcastle with a down goods consisting of a large variety of wagons. Taking photographs in sunlight of northbound trains on lines running north–south would throw the smokebox into shadow — an effect accentuated by any exhaust being blown across by a wind from the prevailing westerly direction. This used to be frowned on by purists but can give a more dramatic effect and is now much more readily accepted.

Left: Class K3 Mogul No 61883 is seen at the same spot with a fast goods train fitted with continuous brakes, commonly referred to as a 'fitted freight'. On ordinary goods trains the only braking was supplied by the locomotive, tender and rear brake van, severely limiting the speed at which they were allowed to run. The 'K3s' were specifically designed for fitted freight duty. Introduced in 1920, in GNR days, they were noteworthy at the time for their 6ft-diameter boilers — larger than those of any Great Northern locomotives up to that time. Eventually some 193 were built, the vast majority of which would survive until the early 1960s.

Right: A down express near Harrowgate Hill in April 1949, headed by 'A3' Pacific No 60065 *Knight of Thistle*, built in 1924 as a Class A1 and rebuilt as an 'A3' only a year before this photograph was taken. The locomotive was originally named *Knight of the Thistle* but mysteriously lost the 'the' during overhaul in 1932.

Below: Two well-established trains, the 10am from Newcastle to King's Cross and the 12.20pm in the opposite direction, had the title 'Northumbrian' conferred on them in the 1949 summer timetable. Here we see the southbound train at Glebe Road bridge approaching its first stop at Darlington, headed by Class A4 No 60034 *Lord Faringdon* on 22 October 1949. When built this locomotive carried the name *Peregrine*, to many a far more suitable name for one of Gresley's renowned 'A4s'.

Right: Like the 'Northumbrian', the title 'North Briton' was given in May 1949 to a train service that had been established for many years. It had a morning departure from Leeds, travelling via York and Darlington to Newcastle and then on to Edinburgh and Glasgow. The return journey left Glasgow in the late afternoon. No 60036 *Colombo*, one of the last batch of 'A3s' to be built, is seen here with the northbound service, accelerating away from its stop at Darlington in the late morning of 22 October 1949.

Left: On the curves at Brafferton, north of Darlington, Gresley 'A3' No 60039 *Sandwich* heads towards its next stop at Newcastle Central, some 50 miles to the north, in mid-1949. The 'Flying Scotsman' headboard carries the well-known and distinctive Gill Sans lettering chosen by the LNER in 1932 for its corporate style. This form of sans-serif lettering (*i.e.* without serifs, the small curved extensions at the extremities of letters) was designed specially for the LNER by Eric Gill, a noted sculptor and typographer of the 1930s, one of his works being 'The Stations of the Cross' statue in Westminster Cathedral.

Left: Inaugurated in May 1949, the 'Capitals Limited' was so named because it linked the capitals of England and Scotland, by means of a non-stop service in each direction. A month later the train is seen negotiating the Brafferton curves in the capable hands of No 60033 *Seagull*, one of the last 'A4s' to be built and one of the first four to be fitted with the Kylchap double blastpipe and chimney. These were known to have a much better performance than the standard 'A4s', as was revealed by being chosen for the 1948 Locomotive Exchanges, not to mention *Mallard's* record-breaking run of 1938, so it is something of a mystery that the rest of the class were not converted until 1957/8. Note the cows on the farm overbridge, wending their way home and apparently quite oblivious to the express passing only a few feet beneath them.

Right: The sun is about to set as Gresley 'A3' No 60085 *Manna* speeds towards its destination of Newcastle with an express from King's Cross on 21 June 1949. The train is pictured about six miles north of Darlington Bank Top station, its last scheduled stop. This photograph is a good example of a camera swing back in operation (see introductory text), the right-hand side of the picture being focussed further away than the left.

Right: Class B16 4-6-0 No 61443 is seen near Brafferton with an up mixed freight in the late afternoon of 9 April 1949. A North Eastern design of 1919, the LNER 'B16' class, completed post-Grouping, numbered 70 locomotives. A few of the class were rebuilt by both Gresley and Thompson and featured outside valvegear, but this example is seen in original form, with valvegear within the frames.

Below: The up 'Queen of Scots' passes the same location hauled by 'A3' No 60074 *Harvester*. This locomotive was one of a batch of 20 Gresley Pacifics built as 'A1s' in 1924 by the North British Locomotive Co, Glasgow; it was not unusual for private locomotive builders to be used by the LNER as a matter of course when Doncaster, Darlington and Gorton had a full production programme. *Harvester* was rebuilt as an 'A3', with higher boiler pressure, only three years after entering service.

Left: Well-known preserved 'A2' No 60532 *Blue Peter* was barely a year old when this photograph was taken, having entered service on 25 March 1948. It is seen climbing away from Darlington, next stop Newcastle Central, with a King's Cross, Aberdeen, Glasgow and Norwegian Lines express on the afternoon of 21 May 1949. *Blue Peter* is nowadays an exhibit at Darlington Railway Centre & Museum, less than four miles from this location.

Below left: The up 'Flying Scotsman' express heads south through the farmlands of County Durham on a late spring day in 1949, still with some 235 miles to go to King's Cross. The train is hauled by 'A1' Pacific No 60132, which would later be named *Marmion*.

Right: Ex-NER 'J27' 0-6-0 No 65836, allocated to Selby, toils up the 1-in-220 climb to Aycliffe with a northbound train of empty coal wagons on 18 February 1949.

Right: 'A4' No 60005 started life in 1938 as LNER No 4901 *Capercaillie*, one of Gresley's last batch of streamlined Pacifics, and was renamed *Charles H. Newton* and subsequently *Sir Charles Newton*. It is seen at the head of the southbound 'Flying Scotsman' on the 1-in-220 falling gradient near Aycliffe on 18 June 1949. Ten of the 'A4s', which originally carried the names of sea, marsh and moorland birds, were renamed after LNER dignitaries. One of these names, *Sir Ralph Wedgwood*, was carried by two 'A4s', the first of which was destroyed in an air raid at York in April 1942.

Right: On a cold winter's day, 5 February 1949, Class A1 No 60141 heads a southbound express at the same location. Nearly new when this photograph was taken, the locomotive would later be named *Abbotsford*.

Above: It is 8.30pm on Midsummer's Day 1949, and the setting sun reflects off the cab of 'A1' Pacific No 60116 (later named *Hal o' the Wynd*) as it heads south with an express from Newcastle to King's Cross. It is approaching what is now Aycliffe Village, originally called just Aycliffe but renamed following the building of the adjacent new town of Newton Aycliffe.

Left: One of Gresley's first batch of 'A4s', No 60116 *Silver King* was originally based at Gateshead as a back-up for the 'Silver Jubilee' streamlined express. It is seen here north of Aycliffe on a late-June evening in 1949, heading a Newcastle–Bristol express.

Right: On 24 July 1946 'A8' 4-6-2T No 9855 was photographed at Gateshead. These passenger tanks were Gresley rebuilds (in the years 1931-6) of the old Raven NER Class D (LNER 'H1') 4-4-4Ts built 1913-22. This example was allocated to Hull Botanic Gardens. *E. R. Wethersett*

Above: Gateshead shed, a major provider of motive power for the East Coast main line, was south of the Tyne at the south-eastern corner of a circle of lines that crossed the river twice, by the King Edward Bridge (west) and the High Level bridge (east). Between the bridges on the northern side of the river was Newcastle Central station. On 20 August 1947 Thompson 'A2' (later 'A2/3') No 518 *Tehran* leaves the north-eastern end of the station with a down express. *E. R. Wethersett*

Right: Just outside the station was the famous diamond crossing, with the lines over the High Level bridge diverging to the right, and the East Coast main line to the left towards Heaton, then turning north towards Morpeth. Arriving from south of the Tyne, also on 20 August 1947, is a train of ex-NER 1920 electric stock. Electrification of Tyneside railways began as long ago as 1904 and employed a 600V DC third-rail system. *E. R. Wethersett*

Left: Some 66 miles further north the next major river crossing was that of the Tweed, which was achieved by means of Robert Stephenson's Royal Border Bridge (so named because Queen Victoria herself attended the opening ceremony in September 1850). It carried goods trains from 20 July 1850 and passenger traffic from 29 August. Almost exactly 97 years later, on 25 August 1947, 'A1' No 113 *Great Northern*, the locomotive that started our journey at King's Cross, crosses the river with the up 'Flying Scotsman'. *E. R. Wethersett*

Below: Approaching Berwick on 12 August 1949 across the 28 arches of the viaduct, 126ft above high water, is another 'A1', this time No 60127, of Peppercorn design, with the down 'Queen of Scots'. Carrying its British Railways number and livery, the locomotive would shortly be given the name *Wilson Worsdell*, in honour of the North Eastern Railway's Locomotive Superintendent from 1890 to 1910. *E. R. Wethersett*

Above: The northbound 'Capitals Limited' is entering Scotland as it passes the border sign at Lamberton on a wet 12 August 1950. This section of line runs along or very close to the cliff top, though in places the view across the North Sea is obscured by cuttings. The train is headed by one of Gresley's 'A4s', No 60003 *Andrew K. McCosh*, which started life as No 4494 *Osprey*, before being renamed in 1942. *E. R. Wethersett*

Right: 'A3' No 70 *Gladiateur* makes an impressive sight as it hauls this northbound mixed freight along the cliff top above the North Sea, having recently passed through Berwick on Tweed on 25 August 1947. Although it became more common towards the end of their lives, at the time it was rare to find a Gresley Pacific on a working such as this. *Gladiateur* had, in January of that year been rebuilt from its original form, class A1 (although strictly speaking it had been reclassified A10, the premier spot having been taken by Edward Thompson for his new Pacific). The A1/A3s were considered by many to be the most handsome of Gresley's designs. In later years, however, their appearance was considerably changed when they were modified with double chimneys and German-style smoke deflectors, as can be seen on the only preserved member of the class, *Flying Scotsman*. *E. R. Wethersett*

Right: Class G5 0-4-4 tank No 67248, seen here, was one of a class of 109. It was designed under the direction of Wilson Worsdell. They were commonly used on trains such as this, the 2 coach local train from Duns to Berwick. It is seen here on the main line near Burnmouth, having recently left the St Boswells branch line at Reston. This photograph was taken on 3 August 1951, only one month before the branch line closed. *E. R. Wethersett*

Left: No 60041 *Salmon Trout* has just climbed the 4 miles at 1 in 96 of Cockburnspath bank and is passing Granthouse on its way south with this express from Edinburgh. *Salmon Trout* was a 'Scottish engine' and was rarely seen south of York. It had the dubious distinction of being the last 'A3' to be scrapped, going to the torch in June 1966. *E. R. Wethersett*

Below: 'The Capitals Limited' is at Granthouse and is approaching Penmanshiel tunnel and the descent of Cockburnspath bank. Haymarket shed's No 60031 *Golden Plover* is nearly home, having covered 350 miles non-stop from Kings Cross. There is now only 43 miles of relatively easy running remaining to journey's end at Edinburgh's Waverley terminus. The date is 13 August 1949, 3 months after this train replaced the 'Flying Scotsman'. *E. R. Wethersett*

Above: No 4557 of class J37 is heading this freight train of open wagons past Prestonpans, a town on the Firth of Forth just outside Edinburgh, on 23 April 1948. The 'J37s', of which 104 were built by the North British Railway between 1914 and 1921, were competent engines, the class surviving into the 1960s. *E. R. Wethersett*

Right: Thompson Class A2/3 No 60511 *Airborne* is heading this up goods past Prestonpans, Lothian on 23 April 1948. It is a lowly duty for a Pacific locomotive only 2 years old, but this class had quite a number of teething problems so it is possible that it had not yet been released for express passenger duty. *E. R. Wethersett*

Right: The footplate crew of this Class J38, No 5919, seem delighted to be photographed as their engine heads this up goods past Prestonpans, Lothian on 23 April 1948. This freight locomotive was designed by Gresley and a total of 35 were built, all during 1926. They remained in service until the mid 1960s. *E. R. Wethersett*

Left: This is just outside Waverley station on a Sunday morning in July 1946. This ex-North British Railway tank engine was designed by D Holmes as NBR Class 795, for shunting and short-haul freight work; the very small coal bunker capacity is evident in this view. 41 were produced in 1900-01 and they became LNER Class J83.*E. R. Wethersett*

Below left: This was a North British Railway design of 1914. 27 were built, all with names associated with Sir Walter Scott, hence they were commonly known as 'Scotts'. No 62424 *Claverhouse* became class D30 in LNER days and is seen here on 6 August 1949 acting as standing pilot at Waverley station.
E. R. Wethersett

Below: A pristine 'A4 No 60031 *Golden Plover* is seen pulling away from Edinburgh Waverley on a dull, damp day in August 1949. It is beginning its non stop journey to Kings Cross with the 'Capitals Limited'. *Golden Plover* was based at Haymarket shed in Edinburgh which had the reputation of turning out some of the cleanest and best maintained locomotives on the East Coast main line. It was also credited, back in the 1920s, with originating the idea of a smokebox headboard for identifying named trains. *E. R. Wethersett*